PEAK PERFORMANCE

SELLING:
How to Increase Your Sales by 70% in Six Weeks

KERRY L. JOHNSON

Prentice Hall, Englewood Cliffs, New Jersey 07632

Library of Congress Catalog Card Number: 87-61606.

Editorial/production supervision
  and interior design: Sophie Papanikolaou
Cover design: Lundgren Graphics, Ltd.
Manufacturing buyers: Lorraine Fumoso
  and Paula Benevento

The publisher offers discounts on this book when ordered
in bulk quantities. For more information, write:

Special Sales/College Marketing
Prentice Hall
College Technical and Reference Division
Englewood Cliffs, NJ 07632

Printed in the United States of America

10 9 8 7 6 5 4 3 2

ISBN 0-13-655358-3   025

Prentice-Hall International (UK) Limited, *London*
Prentice-Hall of Australia Pty. Limited, *Sydney*
Prentice-Hall Canada Inc., *Toronto*
Prentice-Hall Hispanoamericana, S.A., *Mexico*
Prentice-Hall of India Private Limited, *New Delhi*
Prentice-Hall of Japan, Inc., *Tokyo*
Simon & Schuster Asia Pte. Ltd., *Singapore*
Editora Prentice-Hall do Brasil, Ltda., *Rio de Janeiro*

Dedication

To Sandra my wife,
who once believed in me more than I did in myself.
She is my light and foundation.

Acknowledgments

Special thanks to Jeff Seglin, who worked feverishly on
this manuscript to put together a first-rate product. Marilyn
Brandon and Joy Butler both deserve my thanks for the
hours spent transcribing dictation and editing while I was
on the road. My gratitude also to my good friend, Craig
Beachnaw, who was one of the first salespeople to avail
himself as a "guinea pig." He gave me a great deal of
encouragement. In addition, my appreciation goes to Bob
Larsen, a sales manager, who was the first to allow me to
test my theories on his salespeople.

Contents

PART 1   Overcoming Limitations to Sales Performance

Preface

Many people claim the keys to success are goal setting and goal planning. But that is only the beginning.

Success comes from goal *getting*.

The psychology of productivity—a goal achievement system— helps you get your goals. To achieve the results you want, you must first understand the psychology of producing those results:

Why do people succeed or fail?

Why do New Year's resolutions rarely make it to year end?

What are the stressful effects of change?

Why do most people fear doing things that yield high rewards?

The philosophy that explains why we need goals and what goals can do for us is discussed in *Peak Performance Selling: How to Increase Your Sales by 70% in 6 Weeks*. In this book, you are also given a blueprint for attaining goals. The information in this book can help you analyze how much effort will be required to achieve your wants (goals), and it can also help you learn to cope with the stress that might result from increasing your sales performance quickly.

THE SALES PERFORMANCE PROGRAM

All the information is here that you'll need to succeed. The program's philosophy, which is founded on a psychology of sales performance, is clearly outlined in Chapters 1 through 9. The specifics of the sales performance program—complete with charts and guidelines—are included in Chapters 10 through 17.

Changing old habits or establishing appropriate new habits will be an integral part of your sales performance program. Research has shown that correct habits are the gateway to achievement. Habits, along with their formation and modification, are critical factors in goal getting (see Chapter 13).

Part of the program is to become involved in a sales performance partnership (see Chapter 17), since it is much easier to achieve goals when you have to be accountable to someone else and when you have someone to share your successes with.

The elements of this sales performance program are designed so you can produce a personalized program that can help you achieve your goals. Applying the program—which you adapt for your needs, using your personal goals and behavior as a foundation—you can work over the ensuing six to eight weeks to get what you want.

APPLICATIONS OF THE SALES PERFORMANCE PROGRAM

You can apply your sales performance program to virtually any situation in your life for which a goal can be set. Results are guaranteed if you follow your program faithfully.

The successful applications are widespread. People have taken off weight and maintained the loss by staying on diets. Parents have radically improved their children's behaviors. Managers in all types of businesses have drastically improved their own and their employees' performance.

Using the concepts of this program over the past several years, my staff has witnessed some incredible results. *All the salespeople who completed the program have increased their performance and profitability at least 70% over a 6-week period—and some as much as 400% over the same time period!* But more important, these people have *kept* their high levels of performance over many months and years.

HOW THIS BOOK CAN INCREASE YOUR SALES PERFORMANCE

All of us can achieve much more than we do. In fact, right now you could probably name several things you would like to do differently in both your personal and business life. Some of these modifications, if you could make them, could very well mean the difference between $25,000 per year and $250,000 per year.

The purpose of this program is to help you develop a system to assist you in achieving greater productivity and better performance in your current job. The bottom line is

You can achieve greater satisfaction and make more money.

This program can help you make quantum leaps in your productivity and, as a result, in your income.

In *Peak Performance Selling: How to Increase Your Sales by 70% in Six Weeks*, we first examine what prevents you from achieving maximum sales performance. There are important psychological barriers to goal achievement—certain behaviors that make you a slave to your own insecurities. By understanding what these behaviors are and what they do to us, we can overcome these obstacles.

Second, we examine the four greatest fears: fear of success, fear of failure, fear of embarrassment, and fear of rejection. We also look at how these fears may be sabotaging your own success and ability to achieve.

We examine the success characteristics of some of the world's richest, most famous, and most successful people. From these great people, we can learn a great deal about setting and planning objectives, as well as how to make these objectives work for us.

Finally, we focus on habits, habit patterns, and how they affect us. We also help you understand how habits are formed, why many habits are so difficult to break, and how to modify or change present habits or form new habits. Doing this will help you achieve what you conceive and believe you want. We will introduce you to the psychological concept of conditioning and study its relationship to achievement and how it can be used to change or modify your habits.

CHANGE—THE DYNAMICS OF BEING HUMAN

Change is one of the most difficult processes we do. Because it is difficult for most of us to change and to adapt to change, we may suffer from stress as a result of change that occurs regularly within our lives.

Because change is a constant, dynamic part of being human, stress and stress management are integral aspects of the sales performance process. To become and remain productive, we need to learn to cope with stress. Throughout this book, you will be introduced to many stress management techniques.

We also cover ways to keep you from burning out while your performance is skyrocketing and you are increasing your profitability.

Finally, we combine all these factors into a program for your own goal achievement and success.

THE FACTS AND NOTHING BUT THE FACTS VERSUS PSYCHOLOGICAL SALES PERFORMANCE SKILLS

In this book, we concentrate on behavioral or psychological sales performance skills.

Companies often help us in two areas of sales: technical skills and administrative skills. Companies improve technical skills by helping educate us about their product, sending us to school to learn how to operate the machinery, or assisting us in carrying out our jobs more effectively and efficiently.

Many companies spend thousands-of-dollars-per-employee teaching them the job's technical aspects so they will perform successfully. For example, if you are a life insurance salesperson, your company will teach you all about such products as whole or term life insurance policies. Or if you are a bed-frame salesperson, about 10D bedsprings. When a new product emerges, such as universal life or 10F bedsprings, they are quick to provide all necessary data and training to enable you to successfully market their product. In a financial services business, they may also even teach you about such subjects as taxation, financial planning, and accounting principles.

Companies *do not* teach you how to deal with such things as your insecurity in business or how to work with other people. Psychology of management and sales usually isn't covered by companies. Companies *are*, however, always willing to tell you the hard facts about their products and services.

A recent study conducted by Harvard University showed that a great majority of people who retire, resign, or are fired from a business do not leave because they can't handle the work, nor are they unknowing about the product and technical aspects of their job. They depart because of their inability to get along with others—ultimately unable to cope with the frustration and discouragement they face in their everyday work lives.

Basically, companies will tell us we should do it and even teach us how to do it. But rarely will they ever tell us how to motivate ourselves and get along with others to do it.

WHAT ABOUT THE FRUSTRATIONS OF THE MANAGER?

As we stated, companies are also quite diligent in training employees in administrative skills such as sales and management. For example, if we're salespeople, we're probably well-versed in basic communication techniques, both verbal and written. We've also probably learned the importance of listening, as well as various persuasion techniques. If we're a manager, for example, we may have been exposed to participative management.

Many managers are trained in motivating employees and managing products. They are often adept at performance appraisal techniques and methods of forecasting mechanical principles.

It is not often, however, that they are taught about the real frustrations and problems they will face as managers.

THE HUMAN FACTOR—PSYCHOLOGICAL SALES PERFORMANCE

Behavioral or *psychological* sales performance, that boundless, intangible area that deals with the human factor, addresses the issues that companies don't. Using this type of productivity can help us get exactly what we want out of ourselves and change ourselves into the people we want to be.

Developing behavioral or psychological productivity skills is far too often ignored by companies when training employees. In *Peak Performance Selling: How to Increase Your Sales by 70% in Six Weeks*, we concentrate on these skills—the skills that can help you change your life and increase your productivity.

For any questions regarding this book or for information regarding speaking engagements please contact: Kerry Johnson, 24 Sandstone, Irvine, CA 92714.

1

Limitations to Sales Performance

In the last six weeks have you

1. Procrastinated?
2. Not prospected enough or asked for enough referrals?
3. Found that when you finally got around to organizing your messy desk, it was during prime business or selling time?

AVOIDANCE BEHAVIORS—SYMPTOMS OF A PROBLEM

If you said "yes" to any of these questions, you are practicing what is in psychological terms called *avoidance behavior*. Avoidance behaviors are all of the things we do to keep from feeling psychological discomfort.

Such avoidance behaviors, if left to run rampant, can destroy productivity.

As a consultant to businesses, I am constantly confronted with businesspeople who exhibit obvious avoidance behaviors. Some people in the businesses I work with are incredibly unproductive. The issue is probably not that they don't know what to do. These managers or employees have typically spent many years learning their jobs. Their knowledge as well as experience is quite sufficient.

Why don't these people do what they know they should and as a result double or even triple their level of productivity? Could they be lazy—or simply want to avoid the discomfort that the change to a higher productive state may bring?

I recently hired a staff person to do follow-up marketing calls. A basic part of her job was to call people who were interested in using our company's services. Unfortunately, she consistently found ways to avoid making those phone calls. She would exhibit "avoidance behaviors" such as typing out forms to keep track of the phone calls or reorganizing the filing system to make the resource materials more accessible.

While it was obvious that making the phone calls was the most important thing to do at the time, she didn't seem able to do all that I requested. Was this laziness, or was it an unconscious desire to avoid the discomfort those phone calls brought?

The popularity of time management programs, which promise higher productivity, has swept the nation. Unfortunately, many people who spend upwards of $180 to $250 for a day-long seminar afterwards don't seem able to change their behavior enough to reach the promised level of performance.

Why don't people suddenly become more productive the day they come back from a time management seminar? Why don't they make more calls, answer letters more effectively, and quickly get rid of useless pieces of paper on their desk?

The answer may lie in avoidance behaviors. To immediately erase all avoidance behaviors from your life and instead practice the desired time management techniques, you would need to change a great deal all at once. Very few people become that efficient that quickly on their own, largely because there are often underlying subconscious reasons that cause them to be fairly disorganized in the first place. These reasons manifest themselves in avoidance behaviors.

We've all seen avoidance behaviors at work, both in ourselves and in the people with whom we work. These avoidance behaviors may include shuffling cards around the desk, arriving at work late, leaving early, taking an extra long lunch, or possibly even reading a book or magazine on the job.

Pause for a minute. Can you think of avoidance behaviors you engage in in your own life? Do you spend thirty or forty minutes chatting with associates or friends in your office before you get down to the business of making phone calls or dealing with difficult projects? Do you read your mail during the 8-to-5 workday, knowing that it may be the least productive use of your time?

As you might have guessed, avoidance behaviors are not the actual problem. They are merely the symptoms. Avoidance behaviors are indications that you may be experiencing a psychological dilemma on a much deeper level. These behaviors are indicators that you may be experiencing one or a variety of *self-sabotaging fears.*

I like to kid that human beings are only born with three great fears: 1. fear of falling, 2. fear of loud noises, and 3. fear of the I.R.S.—and that all other fears are learned responses.

The four self-sabotaging fears fall into the category of learned responses. But if they go unchecked, these fears are nothing to kid about and *can* be serious impairments to your sales performance.

The four self-sabotaging fears are

Fear of rejection
Fear of embarrassment

4

Fear of failure

Fear of success

Each of these fears is discussed at length in chapters 3 through 6. Techniques to erase these self-sabotaging fears are found in chapters 8 and 9. Erasing these fears is one of the first steps to increasing your productivity.

LIMITATIONS TO SALES PERFORMANCE

We all face psychological barriers to goal achievement. Most of us face these psychological barriers daily in our business and personal lives. These barriers are not likely to go away by themselves because they are often symptoms of much larger and deeper issues. However, to rid ourselves of these psychological barriers, it is essential that we first become aware of their existence.

Before we talk about identifying and ridding ourselves of the four self-sabotaging fears, let's examine some symptomatic behaviors which limit our productivity. The following behaviors are primary limitations to sales performance

*Procrastination

*Disorganization

*Lack of motivation

Procrastination

The first problem behavior—also known as a performance barrier—is *procrastination:* putting things off intentionally and habitually. When we procrastinate, we do not accomplish tasks when we know they should be done but postpone them until the very last moment.

The word "procrastinate" is actually derived from the Latin *pro,* meaning "forward," and *crastinus* meaning "of tomorrow." I'm sure you've heard the saying, "Don't put off until tomorrow what you should do today."

What causes procrastination? Usually we procrastinate because we are faced with a difficult task which we don't want to do. The task might require anxiety-provoking emotional involvement. Or we may be anxiously afraid of making mistakes. So we simply put off doing things which cause us anxiety, like paying bills or talking to intimidating people.

Procrastination not only limits performance but also can promote

5

counterproductivity. When you procrastinate, you might often find yourself asking yourself at the end of the day

"What did I do today?"
"Why didn't I accomplish what I wanted to accomplish?"
"Why didn't I achieve what I had planned?"

You feel guilty because you didn't meet your own expectations. Your self-confidence is threatened. In turn, your performance decreases.

Think of the last 60 days. How many times have you ended up losing a sale or ruining a big deal because you procrastinated—you waited until the last moment, put something off, or didn't do it at all?

Disorganization

The second performance barrier is *disorganization*. Do you find it difficult to locate things in your office? Or to keep track of your ideas? Things you've talked about? Are you spending too much time looking up information that should be at your fingertips? If you were just more organized, would you cease to neglect doing those things you know would make you more efficient and productive?

The concern about disorganization as a barrier to productivity is certainly not a new one. Entire seminars are devoted to time management. Numerous books go into great detail about becoming organized and include ways to think about time and your physical environment.

Surprising as it might seem, remember that, by nature, human beings tend to be organized. There is nothing in your horoscope which predestines you to lack unity, plaguing you with disorganization.

The causes of disorgnization are primarily psychological, stemming both from childhood, as well as from the challenge of coping with a highly complex world. Many disorganized people are in essence still challenging childhood authority, usually that of a parent.

Parents teach their young children that there are ways things "ought" to be, that there is a "right" way to do things, and that a "good" child is "disciplined" and "orderly." The demands parents make and the attitudes they instill in their children toward life deeply affect the child.

Most parents have begged their children in this way, for example: "Jeff, clean up your room." Depending on the circumstances, the child may interpret this demand as an infringement on his or her identity and autonomy. At some point defiance begins. The child begins to resent the parental control. The young person tends to rebel, showing the parents, "I won't be orderly or disciplined." So he or she fights the parents' authority in the belief that order means entrapment or loss of identity, and that disorder means freedom from parents and greater self-identity.

My experiences with my little boy, Neil, are prime examples of how disorder and rebellion towards parents can manifest themselves. Even though my wife, Sandy, asks him daily to pick up the things lying in his room, he usually makes a point of throwing his pajamas on the floor, spreading his toys across the bed, and literally causing his room to look as though a bomb had struck.

At first glance, it seems to be a very natural childhood function to be disorderly. When we dig deeper, however, we find that the disorganization often comes from a child's refusal to do everything the authority figures have demanded because the child needs to establish an identity.

In fact, when Sandy asks Neil to eat a little slower, he sometimes slams his fork down and exclaims, "I don't want to eat anything at all!" A very simple request becomes an intolerable order to many children.

The problem also manifests itself later in life.

When executives' desks are so disorganized that they can barely find things, and their secretary is constantly after them, asking that they clean up the desk, or asking such questions as "Where is the Smith account or the Kellermark research?" executives know they should be organized, but for some reason, they continue to be disorganized, *even though it may be destroying their business.*

Does the executive simply have bad business skills or is he or she rebelling against authority? In this case, perhaps the executive rebels because on some level the secretary's authority in running the office reminds him or her of a parent scolding about picking things up in a room.

The most characteristic way people cope with the emotional conflict of "order–versus–disorder" is by developing what we refer to as an *attitude of compliant defiance.*

Most people desperately want to be correct. They yearn to have their lives organized the way they "ought to be." This is *compliance*—the conscious acceptance of parental standards. They set exaggerated goals and, because these goals are unrealistic and often irrelevant to anything practical, the person adopts the attitude of compliant defiance and says, "The heck with it. I can't do it and I won't." If we adopt this attitude of compliant defiance, it precipitates feelings of failure because we begin to see ourselves as unable to live up to the parents' or parental authority's expectations, which we have consciously accepted.

The Need for Order

What then is *order?*

The elements of real order include a physical environment that is easy to move around in, easy to look at, and easy to function in. Order is a simple necessity for dealing effectively with the volume of paperwork and money matters which we all must confront. Order is whatever helps us to function effectively. We define our particular purposes and create an order—the practical systems that allow us to function effectively and live a purposeful life.

Everyone is capable of being organized. We have a powerful inner drive toward order and clarity. Being disorganized, however, is an avoidance behavior symptomatic of anxiety resulting from the four self-sabotaging fears we discuss in chapters 3 through 6.

Lack of Motivation

A third sales performance barrier is *lack of motivation.* If you answer "yes" to any of the following questions, chances are you are experiencing a lack of motivation

1. Do you sometimes feel that all you want to do is sit there?
2. Do you not want to dial the telephone, talk to prospects, or talk to people at all?
3. Do you find that your self-esteem is diminishing a bit or that you have no real enthusiasm or excitement for the work that you're doing right now?
4. Do you also feel some sense of worthlessness because you're not meeting your self-expectations?
5. In your job, are you avoiding some activities that cause you discomfort?

Sometimes a lack of motivation results from a feeling of complacency. Because of the anxiety the process of change brings, we merely resist change itself.

Beware of "rah-rah" motivational speakers who capitalize on our recognition of our lack of motivation. When they talk about motivation, most "rah-rah" motivational speakers who claim they can help deliver us from our lack of motivation rarely fulfill their claims. Many attendees of motivational, inspirational programs feel just great immediately afterwards, but rarely can they remember what the speaker said.

Limitations to Sales Performance

Recently, I was a keynote speaker at a large real estate industry convention. After my presentation, I got the chance to talk with the program chairperson at length about some of the speakers she contracted earlier in the year. One of these speakers, a "rah-rah" motivational, "positive-mental-attitude" type, spoke at their conference in Texas. While all the attendees seemed to think highly of his speaking skills, they were disappointed that nobody seemed to remember what he spoke about. The people I talked to said they remembered him as being a marvelous and gifted speaker with enormous rapport and enthusiasm with the audience. Unfortunately, not one individual I spoke to could remember anything the motivational speaker had spoken about, nor had they left with any techniques, skills, or ideas they could use to improve their business or personal lives.

A friend of mine, Jim Rohn, author of the book, *The Seven Keys to Wealth and Happiness*, often sees the same attendees at all of his speeches. The popular retort Jim uses towards these repeat attendees is to stand in front of the group and say, "I've seen a lot of you before. How come you're in another motivational seminar? Didn't you apply the techniques you learned last time?"

The point of Jim's message is basically that you can't get motivation from a speaker or by reading a motivational book.

If you ever played little league baseball or school sports, you likely had a coach who gave a motivational pep talk before the game started. That pep talk lasted for about twenty, maybe even thirty minutes. But the performance you gave was the result of your internal motivation, not the coach's pleas. You remember the coach said, "Do your best," but you probably had a tough time remembering anything else.

Many speakers whom you go to for motivation are entertaining and enjoyable to listen to. But until you are able to set a plan for yourself to achieve your objectives, you might as well be throwing money into a pit or a rat hole never to be seen again.

Remember

Motivation comes from within.

Motivation does not come from being "pumped-up" externally.

Motivation is an internal process. Another person can set the stage, but only you can act out the part and motivate yourself.

You are the only one who can change yourself. No one can do it for you. This book is dedicated to helping you make the changes you desire.

2

Self-Sabotaging Fears: How Learned Behaviors Cause Production to Plummet

While many outside factors affect our sales productivity, there are some things we do to ourselves that actually limit our own performance. The limitations we put on ourselves are called *self-defeating* or *self-sabotaging* behaviors, otherwise known as *irrational fears*. These fears are

Fear of rejection
Fear of embarrassment
Fear of failure
Fear of success

To some extent, all of us probably have these self-sabotaging fears. They do more to stifle our own success than a lifelong economic depression.

These self-sabotaging fears are not realistic or rational. A rational fear, for example, would be if you were afraid that your car, a '56 Chevy which has conked out twice this week, is going to break down on the highway soon. That fear would certainly be very realistic. Or if you haven't made payments for the last six months, a fear that the bank might foreclose on your house is rational and realistic. But the self-sabotaging fears we discuss are very unrealistic and irrational. We have all at some time been infected with them.

ANXIETY & DEPRESSION

The symptoms of self-sabotaging fears are often *anxiety* and *depression*. While anxiety may not be a constant overwhelming problem for you, it may arise at the worst possible time, perhaps when you are making cold calls or trying to persuade someone to buy a product or service or to accept your ideas.

Let's say you go into a prospect's or client's office. You've known this person for years and expect him or her only to say something like, "After hearing that presentation, I'll give you two orders."

But then he or she quickly adds a real zinger: "Get out and stay out!"

Would you feel rejected? Chances are you would. But there is no real reason to fear somebody who is not receptive to all of your ideas. That goes with the territory. Such a fear is truly irrational.

A rational fear in the same situation might come if that same client said, "Get out and stay out," then reached for an axe above the fireplace. Your feeling not only of rejection, but also of fear would be highly rational. The truly rational person would have the good sense to flee the premises.

Let me give you a better example of the difference between irrational and rational fears.

I have a very irrational fear of driving in bumper-to-bumper Los Angeles freeway traffic. It usually makes my heart pound faster and gives me headaches and hot flashes.

But about three months ago, I had a very rational fear occur when a friend of mine took me into Los Angeles rush hour freeway traffic in his 1972 Ford Pinto. I called it the "Hindenburg on Wheels." It had Firestone 500 tires. When I told him how nervous I was about the Pinto's reputation for rear-end gas tank explosions he said, "Kerry, don't worry. Ford recalled all its Pintos. They installed smoke detectors in the trunks."

CREATING THE FEARS

One of the basic premises of *Peak Performance Selling: How to Increase Your Sales by 70% in 6 Weeks* is that the fears now sabotaging your business and your personal life are largely self-created. They exist within us generally as a result of the way we were brought up. The big culprits many years ago were our parents, siblings, and friends.

These fears which cause anxiety and depression produce behaviors that are productivity barriers, discussed in chapter 1—behaviors such as procrastination, disorganization, or lack of motivation. Other behaviors that might result from self-sabotaging fears are displays of anger or frustration.

Chapters 3 through 6 familiarize you with what the self-sabotaging fears are, how they affect your performance, and what you can do about getting rid of them so you can increase your productivity.

3

Self Sabotaging Fear #1:
Fear of Rejection

Almost fifty percent of the failures businesspeople experience have been linked to *fear of rejection*. What's more, fear of rejection has a direct impact on how profitable businesspeople can be.

Few of us can cope with being rejected on a constant basis. Most of us feel a need to be accepted by others. Many can't even stand occasional rejection.

Salespeople may display fear of rejection by being reluctant to ask prospects if they would like to buy a product or place an order. One reason for this is that many salespeople feel they have a friendship or personal relationship on the line when selling a product to a prospect. When asked to buy, the prospect may say "no," causing the salesperson deep anxiety.

When a salesperson or negotiator hesitates to ask the prospect to buy, this is clearly a case of fear of rejection. The fear of rejection mainly occurs when we don't want to hear the word "NO."

We all experience it. In 1976, I was blessed with the opportunity to play on the European Grand Prix Tennis Tour. I had a few financial backers, but really needed the backing of one of the tennis racquet companies, especially since they could supply my equipment.

I set up a meeting with a major Sporting Goods company. I remember going into the marketing vice president's office and declaring: "You don't want to sponsor me on the Grand Prix Tour, do you?"

Clearly, my presentation was an unconscious effort on my part to get him and myself to expect a "no" so that I wouldn't get my hopes up expecting a "yes" only to be surprised by receiving a "no."

Think about it. Given my approach, wouldn't it have been difficult for the executive to say "yes" when I so thoroughly prompted him into saying "no?"

I had sabotaged myself because of my fear of rejection.

Even though I desperately tried to avoid rejection with this tennis racquet company, I ultimately did approach another major company. But this time, instead of giving the tennis racquet company executive and myself a predetermined decision of "no," I sold myself well.

I walked into this vice president's office and simply said, "My name is Kerry Johnson. I play professional tennis and I would like to help you sell more tennis racquets."

When he asked me if I had any selling experience, I said, "No. But that is not what I meant."

Self-Sabotaging Fear #1: Fear of Rejection

I told him simply and clearly that I would give him something much more valuable than *time* selling his tennis racquets store to store. I told him that I could sell his racquets to hundreds of thousands of people in the same time it would usually take one of his salespeople to sell one. I explained that I would prominently display his company's tennis racquets any time I played in a tournament. I explained that I would take particular care in displaying his company's equipment if there was to be television coverage of the tennis match.

Seeing a good opportunity for promotion, he promptly gave me nine complimentary tennis racquets and told me to display them whenever I could.

I had become much more clear about what I wanted than with my first failed attempt with the other company. After my initial failure because of my fear of rejection, I realized I had little to lose in taking a bolder approach. I decided to hit my fear of rejection head on.

Needless to say, I was nervous, anxious, and would rather have sucked on a lemon for two straight days than ask this executive to do something I feared he'd say no to. Nonetheless, I found that, even after my initial failure, the door of opportunity has a higher potential for opening when you knock twice.

When I conquered my fear of rejection with the second potential sporting goods sponsor, I was no stranger to that fear. In my teenage years, the fear of rejection had already begun to manifest itself.

I remember one beautiful sweetheart of a girl named DruAnn. I just knew I was in love with DruAnn. The problem was I doubted she even knew I existed.

We had fifth period class together and sat side by side. During the break after class, I maneuvered myself next to her and started a conversation. But as we walked, for some reason I couldn't bring myself to ask her for a date—I was too nervous, too anxious. I would have been completely crushed if she had rejected me by saying "no."

I tried to get up some nerve, but I hesitated, avoided eye contact with her, and stuttered as I tried to make conversation. Finally, I gave up and left since she gave me no great help.

My fear of being rejected by a "no" from DruAnn was so intense that it caused me to behave in an overly shy, submissive manner. My irrational fear of rejection sabotaged my chances of getting a date.

Fear of rejection also plagues salespeople who don't ask for referrals mainly because they simply don't want the prospect or client to say "no." They experience anxiety and frustration just thinking about asking someone for a referral.

PRIMARY AND SECONDARY FEARS

Probably every salesperson in the United States has experienced fear of rejection at one time or another.

There are actually two levels of this fear. One is called *primary fear of rejection*, and the other, *secondary fear of rejection*. Sales People with a primary fear would probably never be in a selling-related business, nor would they put themselves in a position in which they had to try to persuade other people to be their client, do business with them, or contribute money for a fundraiser or other project.

About a year ago in Washington, D.C., I spoke to a large convention of insurance agents. One agent, in his late 20s, walked up after my program and asked if it was true that some people just didn't have the "right stuff" to be top sales professionals. I told him that was probably true; yet it's more a case of having a primary fear than of not having the right talents and attributes.

Examples of primary fears might be

Acrophobia, the fear of heights

Hydrophobia, the fear of water

Agoraphobia, which is literally the fear of being in open places; with this very primary fear, people are even afraid to go outside their homes for fear that something bad will happen to them.

A recent study by the psychology department at New York University found that approximately 75 percent of the U.S. population suffers from some sort of mental illness. Neurotic manifestations of mental illness tend to be anxiety, and depression, which are also symptoms of primary fears.

But a secondary fear of rejection is different. With secondary fears, we might enjoy talking to people, but we would avoid selling to them. We might try to get them to buy our product or ask for a contribution for the new music center only by explaining and not trying to persuade.

To understand how someone might display a secondary fear of rejection, let's take the example of a mailman who is pulled into a job as a telephone solicitor. Perhaps the mailman chose to work for the Postal Service and enjoyed doing so because he wouldn't have to experience rejection. He provides a needed service: he sorts and organizes mail, and when he deals with the public, he does not have to persuade them to buy stamps or to ask for postal rates.

But, let's say we put that same mailman into a highly stressful situation, such as being on the telephone to set up appointments with people he has never met. He probably would have an anxiety attack.

The secondary fear of rejection can keep us from increasing our productivity and performance, and it can limit our profitability on the job. But that does not mean we are in the wrong career. The secondary fear of rejection only indicates we have some anxieties about dealing with people whom we must try to persuade.

A few years ago, some of my researchers did a study on 423 sales or marketing professionals. The study was done to uncover affects and symptoms of primary and secondary fears. *More than ninety-five percent of the sales and marketing professionals my researchers surveyed said they experienced the fear of rejection at least once a week.* We jokingly concluded the other five percent lied.

FEAR OF REJECTION FACTORS: REPETITION, SEVERITY, DURATION

The *repetition, severity,* and *duration* of the rejection experienced are the three factors which affect our overall fear of rejection. These factors determine how much rejection we can handle before we start to use avoidance behaviors to avoid it altogether.

The Repetition Factor

The repetition factor is determined by how often you're rejected. For example, you may be able to tolerate ten rejections in one day, but not fifteen. Or perhaps you can handle eight, but not ten. If you get any more rejections than you can handle, you start exhibiting such avoidance behaviors as

Daydreaming
Pushing papers around your desk
Calling up friends and spending increasing amounts of time talking to people

You may even leave the office at noon and play golf or tennis for the rest of the day. Each of these behaviors is an effort to avoid more rejection.

For me in my business, my repetition factor happens to be dealing with about six negative or difficult people on the telephone. When I encounter this resistance level, I typically start using avoidance behaviors, such as

> I start writing letters by hand instead of dictating them on a tape recorder.
>
> I over-read my mail. I've even read the fine print on junk mail, which is obviously a waste of time.
>
> My favorite avoidance behavior is taking about fifteen- to twenty-minute breaks. I'll chat with my secretary or other salespeople down the hall to take away the anxiety my recent rejection gave me.

The Severity Factor

When we fear rejection by certain people who may be especially intimidating or whom we perceive as so important that a rejection from them makes us feel really devastated, we are experiencing the severity factor of the fear of rejection. On a one-to-ten scale, rejection by such people would register an eight or nine.

The severity factor is also triggered if someone is verbally abusive to us while we're selling. You know the type, the prospect who says, "I'll give you two orders. Get out and stay out."

Here are a few questions you can ask yourself to uncover whether you are suffering from severity factor rejection fears

> Do you sincerely believe that you are selling in a market or at a level below your ability?
>
> Do you feel that you might be working below your potential?
>
> Do you avoid certain people?

If your answer is "yes" to any of these questions, you may be facing the severity factor at work in your fear of rejection.

We can understand how this severity factor works if we contrast two situations. In the first, let's say you're a salesperson who happens to be at home when the letter carrier knocks at your door. You might attempt to get into a conversation with the letter carrier and even start giving a sales pitch. The letter carrier then might say, "Leave me alone, I'm busy," and you would probably think, "Who cares? It's not a high revenue sale anyway."

In the second situation, a professional, say a president of a company or someone you deeply respect, says "no" to a sales pitch. Then you feel the pain of rejection. Because of the severity factor involved in this rejection, you feel psychological discomfort at a higher level than when the letter carrier told you "leave me alone."

Most of us do our best to avoid receiving rejection from people for whom we have a great deal of respect. When these people say "no" or reject us, we typically feel much more severe anxiety than with others.

The Duration Factor

The duration factor in the fear of rejection involves how often we get rejected by the same person or are rejected in the same situation.

If we are constantly rejected by someone we contact once a month or once every two weeks, the duration factor may begin to cause us to use avoidance behaviors to stay clear of those scenes that have a high potential for rejection.

Maybe we've had a boss who has nothing nice to say about our production or performance level. In fact, every time the boss gives us a performance appraisal, he or she only gives us negative feedback. Chances are we will begin to experience the duration factor to take hold in our fear of rejection.

Experts in the financial planning industry, as well as in real estate and other sophisticated businesses, know that it often takes more than one contact with someone to get some business. Often it takes five or six contacts just to get in the door. The problem is that if we experience the duration factor, it will be difficult for us to get past the first "no," negative person, or tough situation. We then would become doomed to spending much of our business life repeatedly failing to find ways to get past the initial rejection stage, rather then being persistent and showing ingenuity in overcoming the repeat rejections and getting the business.

I recently sat next to a woman on an airline flight. Her husband was asleep in the window seat next to her. After a half-hour of talking to this delightfully attractive 60-year-old woman, her husband suddenly woke up and screamed, "Mildred, shut up!" and then went back to sleep.

I whispered to the woman, "How long have you been married?"

She said, "Twenty-three years. Twenth-three miserable years."

I asked, "How come you are still married to this guy?"

And she responded, "I know he will change any day now."

The duration factor in her fear of rejection clearly had a strong hold on her.

All of these fear of rejection factors can be overcome. But before attempting to deal with them, you need to know how you let them start to affect you. How did you get this malady called "the fear of rejection," and the factors that go along with it?

SOCIALIZATION LEADS TO FEAR OF REJECTION

Most of us were socialized by our parents and peers to have this fear of rejection. Mom and Dad would say, "It's okay to talk at home but don't talk to any strangers," or, "Don't talk to people you don't know," or "You should stay away from shifty-looking people." The problem is when you're young, you hardly know what a "shifty" look is, so everyone looks strange.

Our peers socialize us to be perpetually worried about what people think of us. Remember asking your best friend when you were a teenager: "Do you think she likes me?"

We are so desperate for people to like us that many of us can't ever bear to disagree with someone because we are afraid of what they'll think of us. All of this socialization instills in us a deep need to be accepted by other people and to try to avoid rejection at all costs.

But if salespeople never received rejection, they would find their commissions cut in half, because without a fear of rejection and the inherent problems it causes, selling would be so easy that anyone could do it. The point is that if we can get over the desperation underlying our need to be accepted by others—our *fear* of rejection—we can conquer something that's limiting our productivity.

Society has inappropriately conditioned us to place too much importance on whether someone likes us or not, and not enough importance on liking ourselves. *The most successful salespeople and persuaders put a lot more weight on how they feel about themselves instead of how other people feel about them.*

When I first started selling my services as a consultant, I received more rejection than most people experience during their entire career. I realized that one of the best marketing tactics for my sales and management training expertise was to go to existing insurance agencies and work for practically nothing to gain experience.

I had gotten hold of a directory called *Contacts Influential*, which included the names of many of the people at these agencies. One of the ways I promoted myself was simply to make cold calls on the people in the directory. I made as many calls as I could. An experienced sales executive friend taught me to call up and ask for a face-to-face appointment by saying "I'd like to see you Tuesday at three p.m. or Wednesday at four p.m. Which is best for you?"

In most cases, this close was ineffective and simply resulted in the company owner or manager saying, "Yes, I know phone sales techniques too. You're going to have to tell me more about why you want to see me."

23

When one by one, each of these prospects said "no" to me, I promised myself at least seven times a day I would get an 8-to-5 job with a company to avoid the psychological pain I was experiencing. I sincerely believed at the time that they were really saying, "I don't like you. I don't want to talk to you. Leave me alone."

The rejection caused me anxiety because of my overabundant need for others to like and respect me.

Even years after that initially horrendous rejection experience, I still found myself having difficulty accepting objections effectively. But as you are probably aware, when an individual gives you an objection they are really saying,

> "You have not yet persuaded me that I could gain substantial benefits which would mean more than any associated costs."

If you were to picture a scale with a balance point on either side, these objectors would be seeing one side of the scale as being substantially higher than the other.

In my case, when someone gave me an objection such as "We really can't use you for our convention. We simply don't have enough time for a presentation as complex as yours," I felt rejected.

In cases like this I simply began to say, "Okay, please call me next year when you have an opening for a speaker."

Whenever we answer objections like this, we are doomed to fail. I now know that in a consulting business, the chances of someone rejecting you once and using you later are very low. Chances are if they don't use you the first time, you will have a much tougher sale the second and third time. You cannot wait for them to call you. You must keep trying.

In effect, I was really saying to my prospects, "When you give me a rejection, I think you are giving me conflict."

Because of my fear of rejection, I tried to avoid conflict, thereby avoiding any psychological pain if they said or even implied that they didn't like me or my ideas.

FEAR-OF-REJECTION CHECKLIST

Below is a checklist, the answers to which will give you a better idea of the degree and amount of rejection you might be experiencing.

1. Do you have trouble closing?
2. Do you let prospects stall you too often?

3. Do you spend too long explaining rather than selling?
4. Are you unable to make consistent daily calls?
5. Do you procrastinate your prospecting activity?
6. Do you readily agree with prospects' objections?
7. Do you give in too easily to discount demands?
8. Does your heart rate quicken, do your hands get clammy, and does your perspiration level increase during prospecting calls?
9. Do you find it difficult to introduce yourself to strangers?
10. Do you experience anxiety when asking for appointments?
11. Do you experience difficulty asking for referrals?

If you answered "yes" to any three of these questions, you may be experiencing a secondary, or even in some rare cases a primary, fear of rejection.

COPING WITH THE FEAR OF REJECTION

Here are three tips to help you begin to overcome or deal with a fear of rejection.

1. *Introduce yourself to at least one person—a stranger—every day this week.* Those of us with an intense fear of rejection dislike meeting people we don't know for the simple reason that it is not only uncomfortable, but also that they may display a lack of interest in us. But by putting ourselves forward and frankly saying to someone, for example, "My name is Kerry Johnson. I would like to meet you," we will more often than not find that they are as interested in talking to us as we are to them.

   Yes, we may experience suspicion on their part. People often are not friendly enough to introduce themselves to others when there is no apparent reason to do so. But they typically will quickly both acknowledge our introduction and be grateful for it.

2. *Try to trial close at least one prospect each day next week.* By "trial close" I mean saying to a prospect something like,

   "John, how do you like this idea so far?"

   or

   "Nancy, shall we go ahead with this right now?"

   You should trial close in a way that is most appropriate for your business.

People with a fear of rejection typically have extreme difficulty closing because of this simple fact: if the prospect says "no" there is a perception that the relationship is being cut off. Remember, however, that some sales require a very long sales cycle, so the amount of time spent in developing the relationship—replete with its initial "no's"—is a worthwhile investment of time.

For people who experience severe fear of rejection, this initial period of investing time when the prospect is saying "no" is almost like trying to kiss a girl who is leaning backwards. There is no fulfillment.

3. *Try to negotiate for something that you thought was nonnegotiable.* Everything is negotiable.

Recent self-help books drive home this simple fact. *Nothing* is ironclad. Whether it be groceries, dry goods, or hotel rooms, if you can talk to the manager or decision maker, you are very likely to negotiate a better deal.

Recently, I was in Dulles Airport in Washington D.C. I had a ticket to fly on United Airlines to Los Angeles. But I was two hours early for my flight. I looked around the terminal and noticed, on a video screen listing departures, that American Airlines had an earlier flight to LA. I walked up to the American ticket agent with my United ticket and said, "If you let me fly first-class on your flight, I'll give you the business instead of United."

To my surprise, I had gotten very lucky and was talking to the right person. The chief ticket agent said, "We don't normally do this, but the flight is not full tonight. Here's your first-class ticket. Go right on board." Even things that appear to be nonnegotiable are almost always negotiable. That ticket agent could have easily said "no" to me, and I might have felt a little bit silly for asking. I risked feeling rejected and decided to try to negotiate.

Try to negotiate for something at least once every day for the next week.

Don't be afraid to experience rejection.

4

*Self-Sabotaging Fear #2:
Fear of Embarrassment*

The second self-sabotaging fear that can limit our success is called *fear of embarrassment*. Like fear of rejection, this fear is also characterized by our need to have others like us, respect us, and enjoy our company.

Fear of embarrassment is different from fear of rejection, however, in that even though inside ourselves we experience the fear, we may often try to appear to others—in almost all situations—as totally competent, alert, and bright.

Fear of embarrassment involves our ego, self-esteem, and self-confidence.

FREUD ON FOOLISH FEARS

Sigmund Freud, the father of psychoanalysis, based much of his research on a three-letter word that is a basic source of our fear of embarrassment. Can you guess what it is?

If you thought "sex," you're wrong. It's *ego*.

While Freud spent a lot of time investigating the sexual reasons for underlying behavior patterns, he surmised that a male might still, even as an adult, secretly be in conflict with his father or his father's influence. (In adult life, father figures could take the form of your superior at work or even a domineering spouse.) A male wants his own identity, but realizes his father is sharper than he is because his father is older and therefore has more experience. The male fears his father will catch him making an embarrassing error and call him "stupid," or say, "You don't know what you're talking about."

Every time a male hears verbal abuse from his father or someone who reminds him of his father, he experiences a feeling of embarrassment. His experiences a loss of self-esteem; but the real problem resides within his ego.

Males spend lifetimes trying to build their egos up. Often they live in mortal fear that someone might embarrass them and tear their egos to shreds.

In your day-to-day conversations, how often do you hear people protect themselves from the fear of embarrassment by saying things like, "I'm sure you know much more about this than I do," or "I could very well be wrong, but . . ."

Such statements are unconscious attempts to admit ignorance before the fact, just in case we turn out to be mistaken. "I'll give you my opinion, but don't hold me to it."

If we claim ignorance in advance, there is less chance we will make an embarrassing mistake.

STYMIED BY FEAR

Many salespeople find it difficult to sell new ideas or new products because of a fear of embarrassment. "What if my prospect asks me something about this product I can't answer? I'll look foolish."

Or they punish themselves by coming out of an interview thinking, "What a stupid thing to say. Why did I say that?"

If they dwell on the potential to make mistakes and embarrass themselves, they may become too tentative in dealing with prospects, and ultimately lose sales.

A sales manager once told me about a salesman who avoided making prospecting calls. Instead the salesman would spend almost all of his time studying the products. He would bring mountains of brochures, handouts, and printouts containing product information on a sales call. Whenever a prospect asked a question of the salesman, although he knew the answer, the salesman would avoid the chance of being wrong by looking up the answer in his reference materials. Unfortunately, this is both a poor way to sell and a great way to lose spontaneity and rapport with a prospect.

The sharpest, most successful salespeople bring in technical assistance only if needed in the form of a third party "expert." When a tough question comes up, they'll defer to the expert. These Big Hitters are not embarrassed that these experts' may have more expertise than they. They don't want to look foolish but also realize they can't know everything. These superstars are the first to say "I don't try to learn everything. I go out and get my feet wet, but I don't overlearn the product."

We must study our products or services, but if we are in sales we should not let this dominate our activity.

SELL THEM WHAT THEY NEED, NOT HOW IT WORKS

Fear of embarrassment manifests in salespeople who feel the need to educate others rather than sell the prospect. They wrongly assume they can overcome their fear of embarrassment by impressing the prospect into

respecting his or her level of knowledge. They irrationally hope the prospect will say, "I'll buy from you because you're so smart. You know more
about the product than anyone I've seen."

I have to admit that I've never bought anything from the most technically competent salesperson I could find. I mostly buy from the salesperson who can find out what I need and give it to me. If this were not true of
most prospects, technical experts would be the most successful salespeople. There would be no need for sales skills.

I recently bought another computer. The Apple MacIntosh seemed to
be what I needed. So I went to a computer store and asked a salesman to
help me.

He must have had a deep fear of embarrassment. Although he did
finally ask me what I needed, he wasted at least an hour of my time
lecturing me about throughput speed, nanoseconds, and memory parti-
tioning. I'm sure he thought I would be impressed by his technical bril-
liance. I'm also sure he felt a little foolish in a sales situation and tried to
make up for it by reciting a 500-page brief on how computers operate.

The situation reminded me of the child who asked his father where
he came from. Thinking the time was right, the father proceeded to recite
forty-five minutes on the birds-and-bees version of human reproduction.
Afterward, the father asked the boy if he had any further questions. Looking bored, the little boy said, "Well Jimmy said he came from Cincinnati. I
just wanted to know where I came from."

OVERCOMING INTIMIDATION

I often meet fear-of-embarrassment sufferers who use very advanced
avoidance behaviors. They are experts at putting off uncomfortable situations in which they could experience embarrassment. When they are asked
why they're not prospecting to a specific market such as to doctors, lawyers, or top executives, they are likely to say things like "I'll prospect that
market after I finish my MBA." or "I'll prospect that business owner after I
get my CLU (Chartered Life Underwriter)."

Do you fear talking to people who may know more than you do? Or
who may intimidate you?

Not long ago, I spoke to an insurance agent who told me he and a
client had gone to an accountant to try to find out how suitable an insurance product the agent had suggested for his client might actually be. The
accountant not only gave it thumb's down, but also said that insurance was
a lousy product to buy in a highly inflationary, volatile economy. The agent

was so affected by that experience that he made a pact with himself then and there to never again deal with accountants.

Why would this happen? The agent didn't feel as technically competent as the accountant. The CPA quoted from numerous legal statutes and accounting codes. The agent simply felt foolish and was embarrassed in front of his client.

The fear of embarrassment often plagues newer salespeople. Young producers are often asked by their prospects how long they have been in the business or how much experience they have. As a result of their fear of embarrassment, new salespeople may even lie to cover their lack of experience.

A few years ago, a new financial products salesman told me he had exaggerated to a prospect the number of years' experience he had selling his product. Unfortunately, the prospect met the salesman's boss after a few months. When they discussed the salesman, the discussion led to experience. As you may have guessed, the salesman lost his client.

The salesman told me he learned a very costly lesson. The temptation to lie to avoid appearing foolish is very high. If you are working with new salespeople, help them see how valuable they are with their current level of skill and experience. Help them focus on what they do know rather than what they don't.

Many people don't feel adequate enough until they earn an advanced degree. A designation such as CPA, CLU, or CFP, or a degree such as MBA or PhD, however, may indicate an advanced level of extra education a person obtained to serve as a psychological crutch to help rationalize a way out of situations in which the person may not feel confident.

As the name indicates, fear of embarrassment is truly a fear that others may not respect you in the way you want to be respected.

We often try to justify to ourselves why we weren't successful in a sales or negotiation situation. We rationalize to take a burden of failure and also the responsibility off our shoulders. We determine we can't possibly be successful because of a fear-of-embarrassment corollary called *intimidation*.

I had a conversation with a man who was running for a school board election but was clearly intimidated by his opponent. He said he had decided midway through the election that he didn't want to campaign anymore. He told me his opponent had a PhD in education and probably knew more about the education problems affecting the school system. Besides that, he rationalized that he really couldn't put the needed hours into making the school board more effective, and that in thinking about it, it just wasn't something he felt he wanted.

This is a good example of how intimidation or fear of embarrassment makes us rationalize why we don't become successful or why we can't achieve something we want.

Basically, however, fear of embarrassment is merely an attempt to avoid people who may know more than you or people who have rejected you in the past.

I played tennis in college. Shortly before I played on the Grand Prix tennis tour, I had the opportunity in La Jolla, California to play a friendly game of tennis with a man in his late fifties. He had a very soft serve, but he was like a backboard. He could hit everything back.

A tremendous player for his age, I found myself getting upset at not being able to return his soft underspins and slices effectively. I wasn't able to hit any winners or put the ball away. I even got mad at his ability to return so many shots to me. He beat me in three sets.

As I drove home, I remember making a promise to myself that I would never play older players again. I foolishly rationalized that doing so was probably just hurting my game. By hitting back soft shots or balls with a lot of spin, I just spoiled my game, much like playing racquetball might spoil a tennis player's timing.

This is a typical example of the fear of embarrassment. I had decided that, rather than risk being embarrassed again, I would never put myself in a similar situation, even though the fact that he was older had nothing to do with him beating me. I let the fact that he was an older player who beat me intimidate me so much that I wouldn't play anyone similar again.

LEAPING THE BARRIER

If you have a fear of embarrassment, you may find yourself recognizing some of the symptoms just discussed. Of course, this does not mean you are incompetent or won't be able to do a good job at selling or dealing with your clients. It merely means there is a barrier keeping you from achieving what you want.

Your fear of embarrassment puts a limitation on your overall productivity. Fear of embarrassment may be unconsciously motivating you to keep out of situations in which you may not feel as competent or as respected as you want to be.

Henry Ford of Ford Motor Company fame, was once questioned in a courtroom hearing about his technical expertise. He was even queried about his abilities and sophistication level in leading a major corporation. When asked "What is single line depreciation in accounting?"

Self-Sabotaging Fear #2: Fear of Embarrassment

Ford, the eighth grade dropout responded, "I don't know."

"Mr. Ford, how many tires do you buy each year?"

"I don't know," responded Ford.

"Mr. Ford," the questioner asked, "Who was the third president of the United States?"

Ford replied, "I don't know and I don't care. I'm not paid to be a darn encyclopedia. I surround myself with experts to give me the facts. I'm paid millions of dollars each year to put these facts together effectively."

Obviously, Henry Ford didn't have a fear of embarrassment.

One of the most famous people to openly admit a fear of embarrassment is Jim Hart, ex-quarterback for the St. Louis Cardinals football team. After speaking at a sales conference in Cape Girardeau, Missouri, Jim told me of a very foolish, if not embarrassing, experience.

Years ago the Cardinals played the Los Angeles Rams. The Rams had a superstar defensive lineman by the name of Merlin Olson. Merlin was one of the most aggressive defensive linemen in football at that time.

It was third and long. Hart dropped back in the pocket to pass. His favorite wide receiver went deep. The Rams put on a strong rush. He saw Olson toss his own offensive linemen in the air like volleyballs.

Waiting a few moments longer, Hart finally cocked his arm attempting to throw the longest touchdown pass of his career. Suddenly, before the ball release, Olson tackled Hart from his blind side. Hart felt a freight train hit his back and force him face down into the turf. Olson not only knocked Hart to the ground, but, because of his momentum, kept pushing Hart across the natural turf so fervently that Hart's trousers filled up with about four pounds of soil in a very embarrassing location.

Realizing he couldn't reach into his pants in front of 40,000 stadium spectators, he walked backed to his huddle. He explained the problem to his teammates. He requested that the players tightly enclose him in the huddle so that he could reach into his pants and pull out the dirt.

His teammates complied and the huddle gathered more tightly. Just as Jim Hart put his hands into his pants to pull the dirt out, his teammates scattered, leaving Hart the focal point of 40,000 spectators.

Like Jim Hart, after you have a very embarrassing experience, you may develop a fear of embarrassment, leading you to avoid situations that may make you feel foolish. Or you might want to avoid people who think they know more than you. Giving speeches to people you don't know might seem an impossibility to someone experiencing a severe case of fear of embarrassment.

Speaking in front of a group is a situation that is said to scare most Americans even more than death itself. We Americans are so frightened of what people may think of us that we avoid baring our souls in speeches for fear of what a listener might think.

But if your prospects don't hear you, there's little chance they'll buy from you.

OVERCOMING THE FEAR OF EMBARRASSMENT AND CAPITALIZING ON THE LUCRATIVE SEMINAR SELLING MARKET

If you have a fear of embarrassment, you may not be willing to engage in what is one of the best marketing strategies available. This strategy has led to numerous overnight sales successes. It works simply because through it you can prospect 50 people in the time it ordinarily takes to prospect one. Since it is very high touch, it is far better than media advertising and almost equals the effectiveness of a one-to-one meeting.

This advanced sales concept is called *seminar selling*. It is one of the hottest sales strategies around. It is hard not to find a seminar advertisement in your daily newspaper. Believe me, most of these presentations make lots of money.

There's an easy way to get started in the seminar market.

Tom Brinker, who had been a moderately successful financial services salesman in Pittsburgh, Pennsylvania, took my suggestions. He started out simply and slowly by speaking to service clubs like Rotary, Lions, and Kiwanis. His topic was straightforward: "How to Save Money at Tax Time."

At first, Tom spoke at least once a week. As he became comfortable he increased the frequency of his presentations to professional associations.

Tom doubled his business almost overnight. His audience felt so motivated from his presentations that they would go up to him afterwards, hand him their business cards, and ask him to call.

From this point on, Tom was on a fast track to sales success. Tom was asked to be a guest on a local Philadelphia radio show on personal finance. A few weeks later, he was asked to be a regular guest and he now has his own show.

Can you guess what would happen if you could ask a prospect to tune in to your weekly radio show? What a credibility boost! Tom has built his business simply by doing the right things correctly. He started by having a desire to get over his fear of embarrassment and ended by quadrupling his business through the use of seminar selling techniques.

5 STEPS TO GREAT SEMINAR PRESENTATIONS

If you want to prospect fifty people in the time it takes to prospect one, follow these steps. But before you do, remember: *Great speakers are made, not born.*

Most speakers worth their salt have survived one disastrous speaking engagement after another as they learned how to be effective in front of a group. Those of us who have overcome the fear of embarrassment to be an effective speaker have a motto for new speakers entering the fray: "Either you have bombed or you will bomb."

But, ideally, with a little study, you can temper that awful experience. Here are the five steps that will help make your seminar message so full of impact that your listeners will ask you to do business with them.

Step #1. *Ask a rhetorical question of the group and then pause.* You'll get a number of important benefits from using this technique:

a. You will grab the group's attention by asking them to think about an answer.

b. You also let them know you will be solving a problem.

Asking an initial rhetorical question is one of the best ways for a speaker to generate an audience's interest.

During one of my presentations, I ask the rhetorical question, "How many of you have had trouble 'getting through' to a prospect?"

Without exception, not only do the attendees raise their hands, but, in unison, they also say "yes" as their response.

The audience immediately senses a benefit to be gained by listening to my presentation. An old adage in speaking suggests that *if you don't grab the audience in the first five minutes, you may lose them until the last five minutes when they sense that you are almost finished.*

Step #2. *Use your own personal experiences to illustrate your points.* Most groups don't want a book report by an amateur when an expert is readily available. If you give the audience the sense that you have lived the concepts you are preaching, their interest will be piqued. You'll keep their attention much longer.

In a presentation I gave a few years ago, I discussed a concept called *fear of success.* As an illustration, I talked about one of my past professional tennis matches. I played in Rome, Italy against their national tennis champion in the Italian Open. In the second set, the Italian fans, sensing that their hometown champion was losing, threw Italian lire coins down on the stadium's clay court. The umpire postponed the match until the lire were cleared from the surface. Jubilant that I was finally getting paid, I sat down next to my doubles partner and bragged that the Italian tennis spectators were so enthralled with my playing that they threw money in appreciation. My partner told me that it was not appreciation the fans were showing; the lire coins they were throwing were practically worthless. The fans were instead communicating an old Italian warning: *If I beat their hometown boy, I would not make it out of the parking lot.*

That brought on a big case of *fear* of success.

By illustrating my concept of the fear of success with a personal anecdote, I gave the audience a part of myself.

Share your personality in your presentations. Audiences put as much value in this as they do in your content. Besides arousing and increasing the group's interest, you help them grasp your concepts and understand more quickly.

Step #3. *Get the audience to participate.* Conference attendees are tired of being lectured *to* or talked *at.* They want to be involved. They want to be part of the program. One of the reasons why teleconferencing has not caught on, according to *Megatrends'* John Naisbitt, is that it is not high touch enough. When a group is assembled, they want more involvement that just watching a live version of a video presentation. They want to experience it.

There are many ways you can help a group experience a presentation.

a. *One of the best ways to get a group to participate is to intermittently call audience members up to the front of the room.* In a presentation I do called "How to Read Your Client's Mind," I bring at least four people, one at a time throughout the program, to the front of the room to illustrate my concepts. Nothing will do more to increase your listeners' attention than to watch one of their own participating in the program.

b. *Get the group to raise their hands in response to questions.*

c. Better yet, *shed the security of the podium and walk among the audience as you speak.* Phil Donahue, in his popular talk show, has made a career of walking among the audience, microphone in hand. Granted, Donahue is basically ensuring that questions are fielded to the guest(s). But as a result he also involves his audience in the whole process. His success is phenomenal—Donahue's studio audience waiting list is months' long.

Get a roving microphone and walk among your group. You don't need notes. Why not jot down one-word memory joggers and leave them on a front row seat? No one will sit in the front row anyway.

d. *Call audience members by name.* Learn a dozen or so of your audience members' names. Call them out every so often. Every attendee will think you also know his or her name.

Step #4. *Use humor to conclude every major point.* Johnny Carson once said that people will pay much more to be entertained than they will to be educated. There's quite a bit of truth to his comment.

In memory retention studies done at San Diego State University, researchers found that when ideas are associated with humor, they are remembered not only longer, but retained with much more detail than ideas presented without humor.

While you are not likely to be an aspiring comedian, a touch of humor enhances any message you give. Your attendees basically want to enjoy or feel good about your speech, no matter what the topic. When you use humor, you break down suspicion, get rid of skepticism, and remove other psychological barriers that prevent your listeners from accepting your ideas.

I recently spoke at the annual convention of the Internation Association for Financial Planning. My presentation was jampacked with very sophisticated client relations research. Nonetheless, I pumped humor in about every four to five minutes. Not only did the audience respond, but afterwards, numerous attendees told me that the reason they came to my program was because they heard it was enjoyable and fun.

I recommend that you weave one-liners into your personal stories. If they help illustrate your point, you'll be evaluated not only as a good speaker, but also as a charismatic speaker. Charismatic speakers make an audience feel good as well as give valuable content.

A great place to get humorous one-liners is from local comedy nightclubs. I get a lot of good ideas for humor from the young comedians who perform at these clubs. I then adapt the humor for my own use.

Another great place to get humor is from Bob Orben's series of books on humor for speakers. His *Encyclopedia of One-Liner Comedy* and *2000 New Laughs for Speakers: The Ad-Libber's Handbook* include some of the funniest topical one-liners I have ever read.

Step #5. *Never present more than four or five major ideas at any one sitting.* Amateur and inexperienced speakers simply try to cram too much into a very short time period. They end up treating their subject very superficially. Avoid this mistake. The mind can absorb only what the seat can endure. The seat will endure a lot more if you properly present only four or five major ideas at a time.

Of course, the length of time you speak depends on the entertainment value. I'm often aked how long one should speak before a break. A good rule of thumb if you're using my "5 Steps to Great Seminar Presentations" is to speak no more than ninety minutes without a break. If you are not using my steps, twenty to thirty minutes is about the maximum.

Remember these five steps

Step #1. *Ask a rhetorical question of the group and then pause.*

Step #2. *Use your own personal experiences to illustrate your points.*

Step #3. *Get the audience to participate.*

Step #4. *Use humor to conclude every major point.*

Step #5. *Never present more than four or five major ideas at any one sitting.*

A financial planner in Detroit, Michigan, uses seminar selling every month or two. He conducts public seminars on how a middle-income earner can make money on investments. While he is not a gifted speaker, he has learned to overcome his fear of embarrassment.

He has learned that from every one hundred attendees, forty to fifty will become his clients. His average client invests $30,000 per year. All this from a technique salespeople are too often afraid to try.

Make a promise to yourself that in the next month you will stand up in front of at least one group of strangers and discuss your business. Afterward, ask for business cards for follow-up later. Use the speaking ideas outlined in this chapter to overcome your fear of embarrassment.

Even if you can't lead a group in silent prayer, you will increase your business.

Though we might try to deny it, remember that we all face potentially embarrassing situations. Relax, we live through them.

During a seminar recently, I asked for a show of hands from those people who have absolutely no fear of embarrassment. One very proud male said he never had and never will have a fear of embarrassment. I then said, "Pretend for a moment that you took some great clients to a very posh dinner in a very swanky restaurant. During dinner, you decided to use the restaurant's plush restroom. Unfortunately, you splashed some water on your trousers about waist level. If you have no fear of embarrassment, why do you pull your pants up to the hot air dryer for 30 minutes until the trousers dry? Then, as you rejoin your party, you look back and discover you've been trailing toilet paper for 30 feet."

Who wouldn't be embarrassed by that situation?

5

Self-Sabotaging Fear #3:
Fear of Failure

Do you find yourself unwilling to take a risk on a new idea or method of doing business?

Do you find yourself wanting to stay with a sure thing that you rarely change, or stay with a product line you've sold for years, rather than try something new, something different?

Do you find increasing difficulty in setting goals for even a month, let alone a year or five years, down the road?

Do you find it difficult to take others' advice? And, even though the advice is good, do you find it tough to use it promptly in your business?

These are all symptoms which characterize another limitation to your success and productivity called *fear of failure*.

Fear of failure may be a protection device which helps us avoid potentially disastrous situations. But more often than not, fear of failure is an irrational fear that arises when we fear what *may* happen if we *might* fail. The source of it is our own insecurity.

As a great philosopher once said, "Worry is merely the interest paid now on trouble that is not yet due."

ENTREPRENEURIAL RISK-TAKING

Obviously, if we don't take risks, we can't fail. If we don't stick our necks out, we will never get them chopped off. We also will never have to face our fear of failure head-on. But then again, we'll probably never have any great success either.

As an entrepreneur, I've often asked myself, "Why do so few people take risks that could make them millions of dollars? Why are there so few 'rags to riches' stories? And why do so many people stay in jobs they hate or in relationships they dislike year after year?"

These individuals fear taking risks or making changes. They are fear-of-failure sufferers. Usually their thoughts run something like this: "What will happen if I don't make it? What will happen to me if my expectations don't work out?" They rationalize to the point where they will not have to risk failure.

If we declare a goal or an ambition to someone, or tell another individual that we are going to do something, and then we don't follow through, then in a sense we've failed. Or at least we're likely, particularly if we suffer from the fear of failure, to feel that we've failed and that this person we've shared our goal with will think poorly of us.

AVOIDING COMMITMENTS

One way many people have learned to avoid failure is to avoid making a public commitment.

I heard a story a short time ago about a manager who was with a salesperson. The manager said, "I need to know what your goals are for this year."

The salesperson responded, "I don't believe in that stuff—don't write anything down for me."

The manager said, "The company requires that I put something down."

"Well put down last year's goal minus ten percent. I don't believe in that garbage anyway," the agent said.

Will Rogers once said, "Even though you're on the right track, you'll get run over if you don't move fast enough."

But very often fear-of fear-of-failure people don't move fast enough because they're afraid to make a commitment. They fear what would happen if they aren't able to live up to it.

By not publicly committing ourselves, we could feel that we are not accountable. We don't have to explain later on or rationalize why we may not have fulfilled our promise 100 percent.

AVOIDING FAILURE AT ALL COSTS

The roots of the fear of failure are similar to those of many other fears. We have been socialized by our parents and peers to avoid failure at all costs. We are rewarded for hitting a home run, but criticized for striking out. A child feel inadequate when he doesn't bring home straight As or isn't elected president of the student body.

The fear of failure has some interesting similarities to another self-sabotaging fear—the fear of embarrassment. Often, just like fear-of-embarrassment sufferers, fear-of-failure people tend to rationalize why they didn't achieve success: "Well I could have won that sales competition, but decided it wasn't worth it so I quit midway through," or "I didn't really want that account or that policy anyway. I think the buyer would have been too tough to work with."

But people suffering from the fear of failure and the fear of embarrassment also tend to have very low self-esteem and self-confidence. They might tell us how great they are or how easily they sold a house or a million-dollar policy. But they often can't feel worthwhile unless they're able to achieve some great business or personal success, like winning a golf tournament, or buying a $175,000 Rolls Royce Corniche Convertible or selling a million-dollar account.

Even with self-confidence problems, fear-of-failure individuals need not worry because they can learn to deal with their fears. They can take this self-sabotaging behavior, toss it right out the window, and open up a whole new door to productivity and profitability.

HOW FEAR OF FAILURE KILLS PRODUCTION

Not only does fear of failure sabotage behavior, it also is probably one of the most insidious fears limiting their own productivity that most salespeople or managers face.

Fear of failure affects many people. It stems from the fact that we tend to focus more on the downside, negative risk of taking chances than we do on the upside potential.

In case after case, we witness entrepreneurs, like Rod Canion, founder of Compaq Computers, taking risks early on, not concentrating on the negative chances of failing. And the result of taking chances? Canion, with the help of two partners, started a corporation destined as one of the highest growth companies in the United States.

In an interview once, Rod Canion, when asked about the risk he took, simply said he had nothing to lose compared to the benefits he could gain.

To have such an attitude is easier said than done. Most Americans are still conditioned to receiving a regular guaranteed income from their paycheck earned on their 8-to-5 jobs.

To some societies, the idea of taking a risk would be shocking. One of the few societies with guaranteed employment is Japan, where many workers are practically promised they will never be fired. The idea of taking a risk to the average Japanese worker is as foreign in Japan as American-made computers.

To enable us to take more risks now, it probably would have helped if as children we were pushed to take more risks. But we can't change what happened, in some cases, decades ago.

In the early 1980s, my father, Bill Johnson, one of the art directors for Crown Zellerbach Paper Corporation, found himself caught up in a corporate-wide reorganization. A company that was then purchasing Crown

Zellerbach decided it had too many layers of mid-level managers, precisely the area in which my father worked.

My father was given a choice. He was asked at 52 years old either to take early retirement at full pay for three years or stay with the company and be demoted to commercial artist with a pay decrease.

He called me one day and said, "I don't know what to do. I've got two choices, and frankly, I'm worried about my future."

I said, "Dad, this is a 'no brainer.' You've got a choice of either going on early retirement with full pay or staying there with less money and a demotion. What is there to think about?"

There was no question that this was the perfect opportunity for my father to leave and go out on his own. You see, for years he had wanted to start his own graphic design corporation. He always wanted to be a business owner, but because of family responsibilities, he was never able to take advantage of his ambition. His risk tolerance was low.

But here he was presented with an opportunity for a guaranteed income for three years while he started up his own firm—virtually a wide open door to guaranteed success. It made my father nervous. He still worried about failing when he was practically guaranteed protection from any downside risk.

My father had been protected financially for many years with a guaranteed salaried paycheck, so, even though he was offered a plum opportunity, his fear of failure was pervasive.

It wasn't until I pointed this out that he was able to overcome his fear of failure and successfully start his own firm.

3 WAYS TO TACKLE FEAR
OF FAILURE HEAD-ON

If you are experiencing fear of failure, here are three things you can do to tackle the fear head-on

1. *In the next couple of days, take some little risks.* By this I mean take on some tasks or face a challenge knowing full well that failure could be impending.

   Play a card game at which you are not proficient.

   Try to get in some minor competition with your spouse—perhaps something as simple as who can memorize more words in a row.

   Engage yourself in a competitive task at which you could fail.

   While this is not nearly as damaging as putting $10,000 into a highly volatile stock on the New York Stock Exchange, it will exercise your natural phobia about failure and give you a place to start.

Another idea might be to set a goal for yourself of making a few extra prospecting phone calls. You may know full well you might not have time to make those calls, but take the risk. Promise yourself you will make them anyway. Then try to live up to the promise.

2. *Engage in sports competition.* Sports is a great practice ground for helping us deal with our fear of failure. In all sports, any time there is competition there is always a chance to fail. Whether you are bowling, golfing, or playing tennis, there is always someone better out there who could bury you in the dust.

I travel coast to coast, about 8,000 miles a week. This is not a lot of miles when you consider how far my baggage travels. When I travel I still enjoy playing tennis, but because of my pro tennis background my hosts at conventions have high expectations of seeing me play an excellent game. Because I'm very rusty and out of practice, I often try to avoid playing tennis on the road for fear that I might be beaten by a lesser player. Lately I've even made a conscious effort to play tennis against people I know could beat me, only because I enjoy playing so much. This may seem like an inconsequential sport competition to you, but to an ex-pro tennis player who has a big ego, it could result in a serious loss of self-esteem.

Try to engage yourself in a sports competition in which you expect to win but where there is some chance you could lose.

3. *Next time you have a setback in a job or task, tell somebody else in your business or even a close associate about your failure.* Fear-of-failure people tend to avoid admitting their failures to anyone. They are often so distraught by their setback that they hesitate letting others know of their own self-perceived weakness. By admitting your failure to others you will realize that others have been in exactly the same place you are.

We often tend to think of failure as having a worse sting than it really does. There is a fantasy of impending doom if failure occurs. When people have aspirations of starting major corporations, there is always the chance they could lose everything including their home and all their assets. But even with failure, entrepreneurs often tend to bounce back. They often admit that failing wasn't nearly as bad as they expected it to be.

Do these three activities during the next seven days. While they may not stop your fear of failure flat, they will give you a few tools to help deal more effectively with it.

6

Self-Sabotaging Fear #4: Fear of Success

The fourth self-sabotaging fear that limits our performance and productivity is *fear of success*. Fear of success is one of the least understood, but can be one of the most disastrous, of all the fears we have.

The fear of success prevents us from achieving or accomplishing our maximum potential. It keeps us from producing as much as we possibly can.

Fear-of-success sufferers think they shouldn't be doing as well as they're doing right now. They may believe they've been too successful too fast. They'd actually feel better if their success would just slow down a bit.

Fear-of-success sufferers tend to have thoughts like these adages

"It's more difficult to stay on a fast horse than a slow one"

"Be wary of too much too fast"

"There's no such thing as a free lunch."

They tell themselves, "This just can't last." Achieving a lot of success very quickly sincerely makes fear-of-success sufferers just plain uncomfortable.

While many individuals—including some psychologists—think of fear of success as basically a confidence or self-esteem problem, it's really more deeply rooted than that. The fear of success results from having a preconceived notion of just how difficult things are or how tough it is to succeed. When we don't meet problems we expected, we achieve more and produce faster.

At first we feel happy and have a great sense of accomplishment. But gradually, if we're suffering from the fear of success, we become anxious and sometimes even upset. Psychologically we are unprepared to deal with this sudden onset of success. We literally have too much success, too fast.

SYMPTOMS OF FEAR OF SUCCESS

I'm often asked what the symptoms are of fear of success. While the symptoms vary, the experience is generally similar to that of a real estate agent I met recently who told me he used to get a great deal of business by using direct mail. He had used direct mail for more than one year, but then he stopped. I commented, "It's too bad it didn't work for you."

He said, "No, it *did* work. In fact, the effort pulled in at least a thirty-five percent increase in my business that year."

I asked, "Why did you stop?"

He didn't know. The simple truth is that it worked too well for him. In fact, it worked so well it made him uncomfortable. It gave him too much success.

You are more than likely suffering from the fear of success if you find yourself with any of these symptoms

Do you find that your business is not growing nearly as fast as it once did?

Are you failing to follow up on the leads or referrals you get?

When you know you should follow up by telephone after a direct mailing for the best results, are you not doing so?

Our fear of success sabotages our productivity.

Last year I worked with a bright, motivated salesperson who was sabotaging her productivity because of her fear of success. She was new to the sales profession. As a school teacher, she had made $24,000 a year. In her first six months as a salesperson she made $21,000.

What did she make in the last six months of the year? You guessed it—$3,000.

I spoke recently with a salesperson who was a great producer but had switched jobs a lot in a short time. Apparently, each time he reached the level where he was tagged to be promoted to sales manager, he would quit his job. While he made it clear to friends and co-workers that he aspired to be a manager, when the opportunity arose, he ran away from it. He seemed afraid of the responsibility.

Both these salespeople in shying away from responsibility exhibit symptoms typical of fear-of-success sufferers.

We have all either experienced the fear of success ourselves or met people who do. Why do so many people I meet tell me they were four units short of a college degree when they dropped out? Why do so many playwrights disappear after opening night?

CHILDHOOD ROOTS

Like the other self-sabotaging fears, fear of success usually stems from our youth and the messages we received from our parents.

Sheer Discomfort

When I was eight years old, I remember I spent a whole day building a wooden go-cart. It was rickety and ugly. But I thought it looked like a Formula 1 Racer. I proudly showed it to my father who commented, "When you get older, I'll show you how to build a good one."

Heartbreak! My father didn't give me any praise and encouragement for all my work and effort. The sense of accomplishment, the success, I experienced building that cart suddenly didn't seem all that important.

As children we may have been programmed to feel guilty about success. Did your parents ever tell you

"You're too smart for your own good"? (But you had better bring back a good report card.)

"Don't be a show off." (But you had better be a standout if you want to get somewhere.)

"Money is the root of all evil." (But get out there kid, and make those bucks.)

Such negative criticism coupled with conflicting messages not only causes confusion, but also leaves us feeling "Even if I succeed, it's not good enough."

The roots of our fear of success could indeed stem from our upbringing. Likely our parents were middle class, raising us with belief systems and attitudes typical of that socioeconomic status (SES).

As long as we stay within the set SES boundaries we were brought up with, all is well. But when our success moves us beyond our SES walls, we may begin to experience discomfort.

Success may not be what we actually fear. The *trappings* of success may be what frighten us.

In "The Beverly Hillbillies," a popular television show in the 1960s, the character "Granny" constantly made demands on her son, "Jed" to go back to the hills of Tennessee. She was so uncomfortable with her new-found state of wealth that she turned her Beverly Hills mansion into a backhills poverty shack, whiskey still and all. Because her grandchildren, "Ellie-May" and "Jethro," were in a sense still growing up and had not developed fixed notions about their proper socioeconomic status, they loved the new surroundings. They were learning to feel comfortable with their wealth and how to act with it.

SHEER DISCOMFORT

Why do the rich stay rich and the poor stay poor?

The answer lies in *comfort levels*. In the late 1970s, the Carter Administration poured millions of dollars into slum renovations, turning several New York City tenement slums into high-rise dwellings.

What are they now? High-rise slums.

Our family's financial affluence is likely to be the level with which we feel most comfortable. When we experience the fear of success, we may be sabotaging our chances to make a higher income because of the sheer discomfort a change in lifestyle would bring.

Surprising as it might seem, most of us make within 10 to 20 percent of our best friend's income. What would happen if our income doubled this year? We could buy a house in a more affluent area, buy new cars, go on an extended vacation. But our friends probably wouldn't have the funds to share those experiences.

Going to a higher socioeconomic status might entail making new friends and losing old ones. Many of us would rather keep our old friends than try to cope with financial prosperity and its accompanying changes.

Recently during a consulting project for a real estate company, I encountered a salesperson with *too* much business. An axiom of the consulting industry is that you can never have too much business. Once you reach the capacity of your staff and resources, you hire and train more people to take on the added work. Simple as this seems, the realtor's excuse for not attending a necessary educational mortgage financing conference was "I've already got enough business. I don't need to attend."

I laughed and said, "Lee Iacocca doesn't have too much business and neither do you."

What she was really saying was, "I'm uncomfortable with my high success. I don't want to get in any deeper."

She viewed success as troublesome. For her it might have been a disease rather than a blessing. Top salespeople in the real estate industry will often start up their own companies when they have more business than they can handle. But this woman seemed to fear the added responsibility of expanding her success.

Our fear of success may come from feeling that we are not as deserving as others. In many cases, the fear of success stems from our admiration, respect, or even awe for a boss, our parents, or a mentor. In fact, we may feel, "He taught me everything I know. He's much more perceptive and intelligent than I could ever be." But suddenly you find yourself making more money or achieving greater success than that person. We begin to question our success.

The ultimate fear of success results in suicide. Freddie Prinze, the young comedian, committed suicide largely because of his discomfort with his success. He spent hundreds of thousands of dollars on elaborate, expensive gifts for his parents, seemingly in an effort to relieve his guilt at being so successful.

Why did rock stars Elvis Presley and Janis Joplin, just at the time when they seemingly had everything, self-destruct and die of drug overdoses?

Why did Richard Nixon commit political suicide by not destroying the White House tapes?

UNDESERVING OF SUCCESS

Here's how fear of success can affect us

You're playing golf and about to putt on the eighteenth green. Three of your friends have missed their putts. You realize that if you can sink your one-foot putt, you'll win that Michelob Light. You take a couple of practice swings, then suddenly you get a flash.

"Hey," you think, "my friends really should be winning. I've never beaten them before. Why am I ahead? I'm not as good as they are."

If you had no fear of success, then why, when you putt, does that ball go past the hole, all the way down to the clubhouse?

This could never happen, right? Wrong.

In 1984, on the women's tennis tour stop at Amelia Island, Florida, Chris Evert Lloyd was pitted against Carling Bassett. Carling, the darling tennis star from Toronto, whose late wealthy father had been the owner of the Tampa Bay Buccaneers football team, was playing at the top of her game.

She had been playing superbly during the whole tournament. But now, in the finals, she faced Chris Evert Lloyd. True to her tournament form, Carling soundly trounced Chris in the first set, 6 to 3, and was about to defeat Chris in the second set of the best-of-three set match. At 5 games to 2, Carling double-faulted her serve. She netted some easy shots, letting Chris back into the match.

Chris went on to win the next five games, as well as the set. She defeated Carling in what should have been an upset victory for Carling.

Interviewed afterward, Carling admitted she probably respected Chris a little too much. Carling said she just could not see herself winning. Chris's reputation may have been more invincible than her strokes.

Self-Sabotaging Fear #4: Fear of Success

Carling beat herself. She sabotaged her excellent tennis form because she believed she didn't deserve to beat Lloyd. She feared success.

Carling Bassett is not the only pro tennis player to have experienced fear of success. A few years ago I had the opportunity to play a great tennis player named Yannick Noah.

Yannick was discovered in Africa by Arthur Ashe, a great tennis star of the 1960s and 1970s. Arthur went to a tennis tournament in Africa, looking for an individual whom he could help develop into a world-class star. He didn't care about the player's technique. He wanted to find the player who won the most matches and had a winning instinct.

Arthur was impressed with Yannick Noah when he saw him play in the tournament. He took Yannick to Monaco, where Yannick studied tennis for ten years.

I got the chance to play against Yannick Noah when I was in Cannes in the south of France. Yannick was a tremendously talented and gifted player. But after our match, he confided in me that he frequently had problems winning matches when he was way ahead. Yannick Noah told me the story of when he came to the United States to play tennis great, Stan Smith.

It was a five-set match. Yannick was up 2 sets to love, 5 games to 1 in the third set. In a five set match all he needed was 3 sets to win, but he began missing shot after shot, hitting balls out and double-faulting. Stan Smith came back and won 1 set, then came back to win another set, and eventually they tied the set at 5 to 5.

Yannick told me he felt tremendous anxiety and fear. He felt upset at himself that he wasn't playing better, but he realized that Stan Smith was winning only because he was "choking." Stan Smith went on to beat Yannick 7 to 5 in the fifth set.

What Yannick went through was really a fear of success. He was a young player, without Stan Smith's level of experience. He believed he had no business out there winning against a player as great as Stan. Psychologically, Yannick Noah knew that he was good, but he feared beating Stan because of Stan's reputation much more than he feared Stan's ability that day on the court.

In professional golf tournaments, the same thing often happens. A fairly easy putt is missed; a drive goes into the nearest pond or sand trap. Some of the best players can't seem to play well and keep their lead when they're ahead. This isn't just choking, nor simply lack of concentration. It really stems from feeling self-conscious and anxious about doing so well.

Our fear of success may come from feeling overly respectful of a job, or feeling that things should be a lot more difficult to accomplish than they seem.

PERFORMANCE PLATEAUS

When we experience the fear of success, we often find we've reached a *performance plateau*. We may have worked long and hard to increase our productivity, but when we reach a performance plateau, we might find we no longer seem to grow and improve as fast as we once did. Even though we loved what we were doing six months ago, our interest and enthusiasm about our jobs begin to diminish.

We begin to take on the same kind of avoidance behaviors we experienced with other self-sabotaging fears. We might begin finding it difficult to work so we procrastinate more. In fact, even though fear-of-success sufferers *know* they should be working, they sometimes will take a month to six weeks off, twice a year.

All of us tend to have plateaus of productivity for a time. But when we reach a performance plateau, we may find that we do not grow and improve nearly as fast as our experience leads us to predict.

I spoke to an insurance agent about the performance plateau he had reached. He was not achieving as much as he once did. In fact, he was not as motivated about his job as he once was. He also said that he takes about three months off during the year, and works only four- to five-hour-long days. I asked him why he didn't work harder, and he said he really didn't know.

I dug deeper. I found that he was making $30,000 a year. But he had so much talent and drive, I was surprised he wasn't making $100,000 or more.

He told me his father was a teacher in a local school district. The son respected the father immensely. But his father was only making $25,000 per year. The father sometimes worked 18-hour days, read constantly, and worked hard to support the family.

The son felt guilty that he was making more money than his father. The son had only a high school education while the father had a master's degree. The son, the insurance agent, felt it wasn't right that he was making more money than his father.

To deal with his fear-of-success problem, the agent spoke to his father. He found that his father really enjoyed his job. He also realized that money was not an indication of worth or an indication of respect. He tackled his fear of success head-on and proceeded to double his income within two months. The agent now makes $100,000, and grows as fast as you would expect a hard-working, driven, talented insurance agent to grow.

Here's a quick question

If you were a member of the Kennedy, Rothschild, or Dupont families, would you feel comfortable with your income or success levels?

Chances are you would not. In our youth we are socialized to expect to achieve a specific level of success. For some of us, that level may be well below our potential; but unfortunately, we often just stop and hang on.

PEER PRESSURE

Fear of success also results from the pressure our friends put on us. As I suggested earlier, most of us make within 10 to 20 percent of our best friend's income. This can have a devastating impact on our productivity and success, because if we make substantially more than our friends, then they have comparatively less financial freedom than we do. They aren't able to keep up with us. They don't have the same cars or the same houses. They can't take the same vacations. People at all income levels try to find friends with equal resources.

A year out of college, a friend's sales business really took off. He was in the computer business and was a top producer. The rest of us were just getting our business feet wet. I was trying to get experience as a stock-broker and the others were in management training jobs.

Gradually, the computer sales broker became more and more successful. We saw less and less of him, but we all admired his wealthy trappings. He had a Porsche, a boat, and even a small house. He often said that he missed us, but we just couldn't keep up. He wanted to go snow skiing every weekend; we couldn't even afford our own skis. He had a hot ski boat; we could barely afford the gas for it.

He footed the bill for us a lot of the time, but we all felt awkward taking his charity. Suddenly his production sank. His success surprisingly dwindled.

Surprisingly, his setbacks didn't seem to phase him. We saw more of him after that and learned that because of his dwindling income, he had to sell his boat and Porsche.

Over a beer one night, I asked him why he let it all go. He said he didn't think it was worth all the effort. He missed his friends.

What really happened was that success brought on too much change. So much so that the discomfort of losing friends was worse than the added benefits of making more money. He decided to keep his less-monied friends and give up some of his success.

A basic problem that causes fear of success is loss of friends. When you are making substantially more money than your best friends, you may begin to feel your relationships are drifting apart. You may try to keep the relationships together by trying to keep a lid on your income level.

Friends are hard to find and even harder to keep. When your income goes up substantially—much more so than your friends' incomes—you tend to feel stress. Your interests may change. You might want to be with other people in your income bracket. This can put an incredible amount of pressure on you. You may start feeling depressed and spend less time with friends. Or you may feel classic stress symptoms such as loneliness, lethargy, and lack of motivation. If this is what success brings, you may not want it.

Sales managers who employ women as salespeople often witness a fear of success in these women. I work with a popular cosmetics firm employing 100,000 female salespeople in the United States. A sales director for the company recruits highly successful saleswomen and pays them on a commission basis. These saleswomen often do so well that they quickly outpace their husband's income level. All too often, the male not only resents his wife being away working in the evening, but also that her income is greater than his.

A saleswoman in Calgary, Canada, told me that her husband constantly ridiculed her success as a salesperson. He seemed to feel that his masculinity was undermined by her great success. To avoid his barbs, she consciously and purposely kept her income level slightly below his. This was a very conscious, albeit unfortunate, avoidance if not overt fear of success.

BROADENING HORIZONS

In all practicality, when we make more money than friends or parents, it broadens our horizons. Our financial problems are eliminated and we begin to have much more freedom to do things and to meet other people with the same interests and the same desires we have—people who will stimulate us to even bigger and better things.

But any time we change, the potential exists for either anxiety or depression. The change process itself is something most of us try to avoid. This is one of the reasons we procrastinate. Because if we procrastinate, we can't make as much money as we're capable of making. By making less money we avoid any embarrassment over making "too much." We avoid feeling guilty that we're making more than people we respect.

LEARNED HELPLESSNESS

The question still remains

Why do people go through life with these self-imposed barriers, these limitations to their own productivity?

One answer to this lies in something called *learned helplessness*.

Please take out a piece of paper. With a pencil or pen, write your name on the top of this paper. In sixty seconds, using the same hand that you used to write your name, I'd like you to write your name down the page as many times as you can. Now, with your other hand, please write your name on the top of the paper again. Then for the next sixty seconds, use this other hand to write your name down the page as many times as you can.

When you were writing your name with the hand you don't normally write with, did you feel you couldn't do it? Did you feel it was ridiculous even to try? If you answered "yes," this is called learned helplessness.

Just as we readily learned how to speak and to drive a car, most of us also learned equally well what we *can't* do. After knocking our heads against a wall a number of times, we stop and believe whatever we're trying to do is impossible. More important, we develop a self-sabotaging barrier or fear.

RECOGNIZING INVISIBLE BARRIERS— DOWN THE PIKE

The University of Minnesota School of Psychology did an interesting experiment a few years ago. In the Great Lakes Region of the Upper Midwest, pike fish are very numerous. Pike are moderately sized predators which eat other fish. In the Great Lakes Region, their main prey are minnows.

Two psychological researchers did an experiment in which they put one pike and some minnows into a small aquarium. As expected, the pike promptly devoured the minnows. But the second part of the experiment was more intriguing. In this phase, the pike was separated from the minnows by a glass barrier. As you might have expected, the pike hit the barrier with its nose time and time again, until finally, after about 15 to 20 minutes, it stopped and began to swim around in its own half of the aquarium. When the barrier was lifted, something interesting happened. The pike swam into the area which it had been separated from by the glass barrier but, even though it was hungry and had been trying to get at the minnows only a few minutes earlier, the pike swam around the minnows, never eating one—never so much as attacking one.

This famous experiment shows how prevalent learned helplessness is. It shows why most of us tend not to recognize those invisible barriers that keep us from achieving the things we want to achieve. The information in this book can help you eliminate the barriers or brick walls around you. It can help you eradicate the fears that keep you from becoming successful.

3 TECHNIQUES TO OVERCOME FEAR OF SUCCESS

Here are three techniques to help you overcome your fear of success. Because fear of success primarily entails feelings of guilt, to overcome it we must convince ourselves that we *deserve* to have wonderful achievements—that we deserve success.

1. We all have developed conflicting ideas in our minds about how we should act and how successful we should be. Until we change these ideas and make it okay to succeed, we will continue to sabotage our own efforts.

   List 10 reasons why you deserve to make more than $200,000 a year— drive a new Porsche—or buy a new house.

2. *Write down three things you may be doing to avoid achievement.*

   These avoidance tendencies might include procrastinating, poor planning, having no personal or business goals, or even refusing to implement new techniques and ideas. It's important to write down and possibly discuss these things with your spouse or a friend to uncover possible success-sabotaging behaviors.

3. *Write down at the end of each day at least one accomplishment of the day.*

   In the evening reward yourself for that success by eating your favorite dessert, watching your favorite television program, or reading your favorite book or magazine.

A financial consultant in Michigan who suffers from fear of success used similar techniques for six weeks. His annualized income went from $50,000 to $150,000 during those weeks. At the end of the year, he bought a new Mercedes and is truly enjoying every day of it.

While other methods may be useful, these "3 Techniques to Overcome Fear of Success" will certainly give you a good starting point to help you deal with your fear of success.

Everyone does not fear success. We all have a basic desire to be successful and we live in a success-obsessed society. If during your childhood you experienced lack of parental approval, sibling rivalry, negative criticism, or conflicting messages, however, you may fear success.

Do you fear success or are you achieving your dreams right now?

Self-Sabotaging Fear #4: Fear of Success

If we do have any of these self-sabotaging fears—fear of rejection, fear of embarrassment, fear of failure, or fear of success—it does not indicate that we're not right for the business we're in. It only means that we have self-sabotaging behaviors that keep us from reaching and maintaining the productivity level we need to get the things we have the potential to get. In nearly every case, when businesspeople are able to eliminate these fears, they make quantum leaps in their productivity and, as a direct result, in their income.

The rest of *Peak Performance Selling: How to Increase Your Sales by 70% in 6 Weeks* is dedicated to helping you eliminate your fears, and, more important, is dedicated to giving you a design, an approach, and some techniques to help you have anything you could possibly want. If you can lay a game plan for goals—realistic goals—and you follow the peak performance program we lay out for you, you can achieve your goals.

By learning to cope with these fears and cope with the stress that comes with change, you'll also be able to substantially increase your income within a short period of time. You must, however, deal with your fears, manage the stress that occurs when you have them, and find the motivation to achieve. You will then learn how to go from where you are now to where you want to be.

7

What Self-Sabotaging Fears Can Do to Your Sales Performance

All of the self-sabotaging fears—of rejection, embarrassment, failure, and success—work hard to stop us from performing at peak production levels. In fact, sales management experts have found the biggest block to productivity is not our skill level or what we know about sales. It is more likely how much time we spend sabotaging our own production.

How much business could you handle if you stopped blocking your productivity with self-sabotaging fears? How much time do you waste reorganizing your desk or prioritizing phone calls or sitting in your chair at work thinking about what you are about to say to someone? How much anxiety do you feel in getting your confidence up to do "battle" in sales?

Too many people let their anxiety stump them. They either sit at their chair looking at the telephone or rationalize their way out of working effectively. It might be difficult to rationalize making excuses to the sales manager, but compared to the anxiety some people face about prospecting clients, it's relatively easy.

A salesperson might say to his or her manager, "I really can't make a phone call this afternoon. I have to prepare my appointment with my prospect tomorrow."

Or they may simply say, "I know that my prospect might be in this afternoon."

Or, "This is a bad time to call him. He's obviously busy."

Individuals who have a high level of *self-esteem* tend to let self-sabotaging fears hit them without much impact. Sales managers who are looking for a successful producer not only look for someone with high self-esteem, but also look for someone who is hungry. They believe that someone who is financially well off may not have the same level of determination to produce.

Too much anxiety about tackling a tough job may be paralyzing you and keeping you on the defensive so that you avoid putting yourself in situations where you may get rejected and feel failure. But a hunger to achieve and succeed is probably helpful to get salespeople out of their armchairs to see somebody.

SELF-ESTEEM

To understand how self-esteem works, think of the gold vault at Fort Knox. Gold is expensive whether it inflates in value daily, monthly, or even yearly. When the United States' economy was linked to the gold standard, basically it meant that the more gold it had, the more paper money it could produce. The less gold it had, the worse off its economy was. The dollar was pegged to the value of gold. This concept parallels how self-esteem—"the gold in our mind"—works.

In your mind, you set the value of your self-esteem. The more value you place on yourself, the more "gold" you deposit in your mind.

Real gold is put into the Fort Knox vault on deposit. Gold can also be withdrawn, but only at the same value. So gold worth $100 an ounce when it is deposited can only be withdrawn at $100 an ounce.

If you continually think of yourself as having difficulty making phone calls, you are actually making deposits of very low worth into your mental vault. When the time comes to make withdrawals, to perform a skill such as making prospecting calls, you will withdraw skills that you've attached a low value to. In other words, the gold you withdraw from your mental vault would have the same low value as it had when you deposited it.

Other people can influence the value of your mental gold with their compliments, strokes, and praises. But it's your own self-appraisals, your own self-esteem, that will trigger the self-sabotaging fears that can keep you from achieving your maximum potential performance.

Individuals with high self-esteem and high self-worth place an extremely high value on their mental gold. It is as if they had trained a guard to stand in the doorway of their mental vault. This guard rejects gold that has little value attached to it (perhaps as a result of negativity, self-depreciation, or harsh self-reproach) and only allows deposits that have a very high worth.

UNDERSTANDING OUR OWN BEHAVIOR

Sigmund Freud, in his famous works on psychoanalysis, determined that the basic personalities human beings possess were developed between the ages of two and seven years. In fact, Jean Piaget, the developmental psychological researcher, substantiates that this is when the imprinting process—when children largely take on the characteristics of their parents—takes place. If the parents have a tendency to be overweight during the first two to seven years of the child's development, the child may also find itself unconsciously gaining weight as well. If the parents smoked in the house when the child was young, the child will have a strong tendency to smoke in later life.

While many "experts" will tell you that people can change any time they want if there's enough motivation to do it, it is just not that simple.

Basic behavior changes like stopping smoking can take an enormous amount of work. Your psychological fears—be they of failure, rejection, success, or embarrassment—may be equally difficult to change.

Marriage counselors often agree that second marriages are rarely more successful and problem-free than first marriages. When the female, for example, divorces the male for reasons such as lack of affection, she may do her best to marry a male who is affectionate. Unfortunately, she may find that in the second marriage there are different but equally severe problems with her husband. She needs to focus on the real issue—her own behavior—and only secondarily on the behavior of her spouse.

The same is true of self-sabotaging fears. Because of my own fear of embarrassment, I have had an extremely hard time speaking in front of audiences. This is fairly difficult to understand since I make a substantial part of my living by speaking professionally to more than 1,000 people every week. For two straight years, however, I had difficulty sleeping for even ten minutes the night before a presentation. My fear of the audience disliking my message or me was extreme.

Six years later, I am still speaking to audiences around the United States. I have not had difficulty sleeping for a few years now. I was able to deal with my fear simply by hitting my head against a brick wall and eventually knocking down the wall.

But behaviors are difficult to change completely. Even though I learned to cope with my fear of audiences and public speaking, I've still not erased it totally.

Recently I was asked by the president of my church's Sunday School class to do a nine-week lecture series on parenting. I realized I would have to go back to psychological manuals and books on the subject to gain a better understanding of how parents should deal with their children to bring them up as happy, responsible, and ethical high achievers.

I spent two to three weeks preparing for my presentation. But the day I was to speak to a group of seventy in the Sunday School class was also the day I became reacquainted with my fear of speaking.

The night before my presentation I was scared to death. I went to bed at 10:30, but probably didn't get to sleep until almost 3 a.m. I wasn't worried about the content as much as I was concerned about doing a good job in front of people who knew me, and in many cases, knew me very well. My self-sabotaging fear of embarrassment returned. I sat in the chair in the Sunday School class 20 minutes before I was introduced, feeling my hands become clammy and my heart pound like a bass drum. When I was introduced, I walked to the front and, as I spoke, even felt my voice quaking and quivering; frankly, I also knocked the speaker stand down within 30 seconds of starting my speech.

Obviously, I had not lost my fear. But professionally, I had learned to cope with it.

REASONS FOR SABOTAGING YOURSELF

You already know that fears often produce avoidance behaviors. Avoidance behaviors, as stated earlier, are those behaviors we engage in to keep from feeling the painful effects of fear and anxiety. For example, being overly perfectionistic is an avoidance behavior. If you spend an inordinate amount of time typing a letter or writing an article and, as a result, have no time to make phone calls or straighten out a problem with a staff person, you are using an avoidance behavior to avoid a possible conflict.

In their book, *Treat Your Ego in Four Hours*, Tom Ruske, M.D. and Randolph Read, M.D. state that everyone uses avoidance behaviors or *escapes* as tools for everyday life. These escapes include behaviors such as sleeping, drinking, eating, or even reading at inappropriate times. They are not an indication of mental illness but simply an indication of an inability to cope.

Doctors Ruske and Read also suggest that we sometimes sabotage ourselves to achieve an unconscious, hidden goal. For example, when people are overweight, they may not gain weight simply because they like to eat. People who tend to be fat may use their physical shape to avoid putting themselves in positions where they may feel some discomfort

> If you are overweight, you might not be good-looking. You won't have to spend much time searching through stores to spend money on expensive, trendy clothing.
>
> You can stay at home more often because you are asked to go out less.
>
> You may have fewer friends, because in our society people tend to pay more attention and engage in conversation with attractive people.
>
> You also might lose some self-respect and find it more advantageous to let other people take pity on you.

The real benefit, then, to being overweight is that one gains protection from relationships that might be too demanding.

Many pyschotherapists believe that women overeat to be able to avoid rejection from men. If they spend hours and hours each week exercising, grooming themselves, shopping for clothes, and dieting, they are, in effect, pushing themselves to be more physically attractive and available to the opposite sex. After all their work, if men still don't reward them for their effort by asking them out or paying a lot of attention to them, women may feel even more deeply rejected than when they were overweight. Why not avoid or risk rejection by simply gaining weight?

In sales, a salesperson may react similarly and think, Why risk rejection on the telephone? Simply don't make the phone calls.

Odd as it may sound, people who avoid making calls when it is part of their job may be doing so because of the benefits they receive. One benefit is not giving the person on the other end of the line a chance to speak harshly to you. That secretary might not give you a tough time on the telephone. She won't have the chance to screen you and decide whether she will let you talk to the decision maker.

A benefit of less productivity is having to spend less time at the office and being able to spend more time at home. Or perhaps the benefit is letting friends and acquaintances realize you're just like they are. You don't have to face the problem of making more money than your friends do. If you don't make a lot of money, friends and relatives may expect less from you. Relatives don't come by to ask for money. You won't have to spend time talking to CPAs and financial planners to try to shelter your income from taxes.

WEIGHING THE BENEFITS OF TACKLING FEARS

Take some time now to list at least ten benefits you can think of for not doing something you think you are afraid of. Whether it involves the fear of rejection, embarrassment, failure, or success, list ten reasons you could have for using an avoidance behavior to achieve an unconscious hidden goal.

An avoidance behavior I use when I fear speaking, for example, is to not call the meeting planner to commit to a speaking date.

If I don't call the meeting planner

1. I won't have to lose sleep the night before.
2. I won't experience anxiety thinking about the presentation.
3. My anxiety won't increase when my wife asks me what I am going to speak about in the program.
4. I won't have to go to the library and spend four or five hours' research to tailor my topic to the group's needs.
5. I won't have to vividly recall my sleepless nights.
6. I won't be distracted from doing other activities because of a preoccupation with the upcoming presentation.
7. I won't have to face embarrassing questions after my presentation.

8. I won't have to deal with the group if they don't like my presentation.
9. I won't have to worry about making future presentations to the same group.
10. I won't have to make future choices about whether or not I should stay in my current career.

By listing the benefits of using avoidance behaviors, I am putting a worth on those benefits. By doing this, I then can weigh them against the *favorable* benefits of calling a meeting planner.

Next, I would like you to write down the favorable benefits of doing something you might typically be afraid to do. For, example, if you shy away from making prospecting calls, make a list of the positive benefits you get from making the calls.

The favorable benefits I might get from calling that meeting planner to commit to a date might include the following

1. I'd make some money from the speech.
2. I'd be able to travel to a different part of the country.
3. I'd get applause after my presentation.
4. People would flock to the front of the room asking for autographed copies of my book after the presentation.
5. I might receive more respect from my family.
6. I'd feel a greater sense of self-worth.
7. I could save the money to buy a nicer car.
8. I could use the money to feed my family.
9. I'd feel good about being able to provide for my family.
10. I'd enjoy my work more.

Once you have written down the benefits of *not doing* an activity, as well as the benefits of *doing* it, you should be able to weigh one against the other to decide if it is really worth it to you to go ahead and do that activity. Because you're basing the decision on knowledge of both sides of the issue, this method is a very *cognitive approach* to determining whether or not a behavior is worthwhile.

All activities have a plus and a minus side. We've all sat down at one time or another and listed the benefits versus the drawbacks of doing something. Maybe it was accepting a lucrative job offer with a less than stable startup company. Or maybe it was deciding whether or not to go back to school. To make intelligent decisions about something we have to know the downside as well as the upside.

Weighing the Benefits of Tackling Fears

If you refuse to weigh your options, you are simply saying to yourself that you have absolutely no control over your own behavior. On the other hand, if you convince yourself that everything you do is in some way useful to you in achieving a successful outcome, you then will be taking on more responsibility for your actions. You'll be able to make clear business and personal decisions.

If you decide *not* to make prospecting phone calls, at least you will be aware of the benefits you think you are receiving as a result.

When I worked as a consultant for a major computer firm, I came across an individual who was an average producer selling large mainframe computer systems. His name was Mel. I asked Mel one day, "When you look at ways to increase production, have you found anything about the job that motivates you?"

Mel confided to me that money was not all that important to him. What he really wanted was a chance to move up in the company. When I began working with him to outline a game plan for strategizing his career to get to the top of his company, he stopped me abruptly. He said, "When I really think about, I guess I really don't want my boss's job. My boss has no power, lots of problems, and too many conflicts in his career. I really don't want that."

Mel was actually avoiding increasing his sales production because he did not want to risk being promoted. He eased up on his productivity because he had perceived definite benefits from not achieving superstar sales production. If his sales rose too high, he would likely be promoted, get more money, and be pushed into a managerial position he didn't want. For Mel, the promotion and money did not outweigh the drawbacks of the managerial position.

Are you like Mel?

Have you consciously or unconsciously decided that you do not want the rewards and problems that success brings?

Are you artificially keeping your production low by avoiding phone calls, spending a lot of social time with associates in your office, coming to work late, leaving early, or not reading books that could help develop your sales skills?

Is this an unconscious strategy you are using to achieve your own preset goal?

After you have weighed the cost of not changing against the benefits of changing, you can then decide whether to go through what could be a painful process of reworking certain behaviors in your own personality.

Just like Mel, the computer salesman, you may realize that the action involved in changing is not so difficult, but the results are not what you want. In that case, you would simply stay where you are.

On the other hand, if you find that the benefits far outweigh the drawbacks, then you must determine how you want to change.

HOW DO YOU WANT TO CHANGE?

You should ask yourself the following questions

1. When do you want to change?
2. What is prompting you to change?
3. What specifically would you like to change?
4. What are the avoidance behaviors you may be using to avoid changing?

Change involves effort and risk. But if you have enough desire to change, that effort won't seem as difficult, and the risk won't seem as fearsome. Rarely do any of us map out these four steps when we want to change behavior patterns, but if we really want to change, looking hard at our answers to these questions will make the process easier.

Bethany, a real estate agent I worked with, wanted to change her behavior so she could make more money. She answered the questions this way

1. She wanted to change within 30 days.
2. She was tired of netting only a few hundred dollars per month over her expenses.
3. She wanted to be able to knock on at least ten doors each day and ask people if they wanted to list their homes.
4. She realized that the avoidance behavior she was using was to rationalize that she was too busy showing houses or doing paperwork in her office to knock on prospects' doors.

Once Bethany knew when she wanted to change, exactly what was prompting her to change, as well as the avoidance behavior she might be using to sabotage herself, she was well-armed to make that change.

PLAY THERAPY

One of the ways people sabotage their productivity levels is simply by taking themselves too seriously. They are paralyzed when it comes to making decisions because they put too much importance on the possible outcome of their decisions. Remember: the decisions you make on a daily basis will not substantially make or break your sales career. Your career is the coordination of weeks, months, and years of effort. The actions of only very few of us have as huge an impact as those of the President of the United States who, by doing something as innocuous as forgetting to shake the hand of a dignitary from another nation, could align that other nation with a communist power.

Play therapy is a means, not of making a game out of what we do, but of taking frequent "fun" breaks throughout the day. It is far more difficult to use avoidance behaviors or feel the stressful effect of our fears if we enjoy ourselves during the day.

I recently spoke to a salesperson who started every phone conversation with a prospect by talking about something nice or humorous he heard in the secretary's voice who transferred him to the prospect. For example, "Mr. Kemper, I really enjoyed talking to your secretary. On the telephone, she sounds like a cross between Linda Evans from "Dynasty" and Linda Ellerbee, the news correspondent with ABC News."

Because of their relationship to their secretaries, when they hear this, prospects will typically laugh or at least feel like the ice has been broken a bit.

When you use humor with prospects, some of the pressure of the situation disappears. You'll have less of a chance of rejection, and a more receptive audience for your proposal.

When you can have fun in your conversations with prospects, you greatly increase the chance that you will call another directly afterward.

You should not only make sales situations fun, but also try to give yourself *play breaks*. Play breaks help take some of the pressure off during stressful situations in which you might be using avoidance behaviors. In these cases, take a brief break. You might try to remember an amusing film you saw or an interesting radio commercial you've just heard on your company's internal music system. You might observe a bit of ridiculousness in the way a person walks through the hallway. Or you may, as I do, pick up a sheet of paper, walk to an associate's desk and tell him or her your favorite joke.

Some people may see taking time out from making phone calls as being undisciplined. But if it relaxes you and, as a result, makes you more productive, play breaks are a great way to take the pressure off and enjoy your work day.

Play breaks don't require a particular methodology as much as they do an attitude of moderation. An essential element of effective play breaks is to have enough discipline to keep them short and to stop the play break from itself becoming an avoidance behavior.

Used in small amounts, sprinkling play breaks throughout your day is much like putting a pinch of salt on mashed potatoes. You can greatly enhance the enjoyability of your meal or of your work.

3-MINUTE PHOBIA CURE

One of the most interesting and provacative ways to deal with your sabotaging fears is what psychotherapists Richard Bandler and John Grinder call their "3- to 6-Minute Phobia Cure." Bandler and Grinder, through a process called *Neuro-Linguistic Programming*, have for years confounded traditional psychotherapists. They believe that many people with fears and phobias unconsciously allow their psychotherapists to lull them into weeks, months, and even years of counseling. At the rate of between $75 and $100 an hour it has become very lucrative for the psychotherapist. But Bandler and Grinder believe that people with fears have simply not allowed themselves to dissociate from feelings of past experiences. For example, when they picture their feared activity, such as driving on the freeway, they also imagine the panic they once felt some years earlier. They avoid this panic by not driving on the freeway, or, in some cases, not driving at all.

Bandler's and Grinder's phobia cure simply helps the fear sufferer to associate with pleasant memories, and become dissociated from unpleasant memories. While this may sound very simple, the hard part is to do it often enough, with enough concentration, that your brain molds the new, "fear-less" habit. Then the mind automatically triggers only pleasant memories and forgets unpleasant ones.

They report that the "3-Minute Phobia Cure" is one of the quickest and most persuasive ways of changing people and their specific behaviors. Here is how it works

> If you have a fear of being in elevators, for example, the first thing to do is imagine you're sitting in the middle of a movie theatre. On the screen, you see a black-and-white photograph of yourself in the situation you experienced *just before* you had the initial phobic response or anxiety standing outside the elevator.

The next step in this phobia cure is to imagine yourself not in the middle of the movie theatre, but in the projection booth of the same theatre. Here, you can watch yourself still sitting in the middle of the theatre watching yourself in a still photograph on the screen.

The next step is to turn the photograph into a black-and-white movie. Back in the middle of the theatre, you watch this film of yourself outside the elevator, walking into the elevator, and all events until the end of the unpleasant experience.

Bandler and Grinder suggest that when you get to the end of the movie, you stop again on a final frame in the film, and then suddenly jump inside the picture and roll the movie backward. Everybody and everything in the movie walks backwards, runs backwards—runs totally in reverse. You are basically rewinding the film, except that you are in the film watching yourself moving backwards through the elevator. The only rule in running the movie backwards is you must imagine it in color, and take only one to two seconds to do it.

In fact, in Bandler's and Grinder's phobia cure you distance yourself from your own actions by imagining that you're watching yourself watch yourself on a screen in a black-and-white movie of the entire unpleasant experience. You then kind of "undo" the experience by imagining yourself jumping inside the picture and then running it rapidly backwards in color. In a way you are ridiculing your phobic anxiety response in the elevator by imagining the experience as a sort of slapstick sight gag. But this method may also give you some relief from anxiety. By the end of this phobia cure, you imagine yourself in color rapidly reliving this event from its point of highest anxiety backward to the point of no anxiety. You're going very quickly from very bad to very good.

This cure could also work with telephone calls. If you have a horrible fear of calling people on the telephone, you could simply imagine yourself in the middle of the movie theatre, seeing up on the screen a black-and-white photograph of yourself just before making a phone call which gives you very high anxiety.

Then imagine yourself in the projection booth, watching yourself watching yourself staring at the telephone about to make a call. Then, turn that snapshot into a black-and-white movie and watch the movie progress from you staring at the telephone to making the telephone call, having a conversation, feeling the anxiety, and eventually hanging up the telephone.

Then stop the movie and stare at it as if it were a slide photograph. See yourself jumping inside this slide, then run the movie backwards, in color, at an extremely rapid rate.

You are actually becoming disassociated from the anxiety of the phobic experience of making that telephone call. This phobia cure has been used with great success. Many people have absolutely no symptoms of the phobia after the treatment, as well as no symptoms for weeks and months afterward.

The authors of the treatment, John Grinder and Richard Bandler, have saved thousands of people who wished to overcome specific phobias not only time but also as much as $70,000 to $100,000 in psychotherapeutic costs. It is such a simple technique that it is exceptional.

Try it the next time you feel any anxiety about making a telephone call, seeing somebody face-to-face, speaking in front of a group, or when you find that any of the sabotaging fears—rejection, embarrassment, failure, or success—rear their ugly heads.

The benefits may be enormous; the risk is minimal.

8

How to Eliminate Your Sales Performance Barriers: Using SUDS to Wash Away Self-Sabotaging Fears

Our sales performance problems stem from experiencing any, some, or all of the four self-sabotaging fears

Fear of rejection
Fear of embarrassment
Fear of failure
Fear of success

We avoid achieving our maximum potential because of the anxiety these fears bring us.

In extreme cases, our fears overwhelm us. Like the person in chapter 7 who used Bandler and Grinder's "3-Minute Phobia Cure," some people are deathly afraid of riding in elevators. They're terribly frightened of being suspended in a box going up and down in a building. All they can envision is a wire breaking or a motor malfunctioning. They see themselves kissing their nice lives good-bye.

The real reason people feel upset when riding elevators is not because they dislike the convenience of elevators or moving up and down rapidly. The real reason they fear elevators is they fear the horrible anxiety or extreme discomfort they associate with riding in elevators. Even though the fear of riding in an elevator is really irrational, it still can bring on anxiety.

If we don't learn to live with our own anxiety, we'll never reach our full potential—our maximum sales productivity level. We'll continue to avoid prospecting for new clients or asking for referrals. We will literally avoid success.

But please be assured. There are indicators we can use to let us know when we are sabotaging our own sales performance. These indicators let us know when we're suffering from self-sabotaging fears and when anxiety has taken over and limits our performance.

THE SUDS SCALE

One such measurement is called the *SUDS Scale*. SUDS stands for "Subjective Unit of Discomfort Scale." Figure 8.1 features the SUDS Scale complete with its different levels of discomfort.

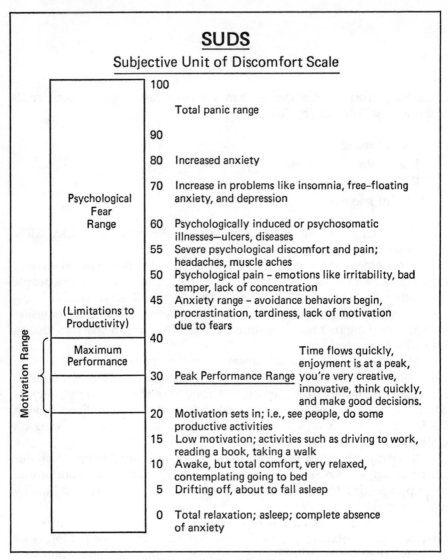

SUDS
Subjective Unit of Discomfort Scale

Motivation Range			
		100	
			Total panic range
	Psychological Fear Range	90	
		80	Increased anxiety
		70	Increase in problems like insomnia, free–floating anxiety, and depression
		60	Psychologically induced or psychosomatic illnesses—ulcers, diseases
		55	Severe psychological discomfort and pain; headaches, muscle aches
		50	Psychological pain – emotions like irritability, bad temper, lack of concentration
	(Limitations to Productivity)	45	Anxiety range – avoidance behaviors begin, procrastination, tardiness, lack of motivation due to fears
		40	
	Maximum Performance		Time flows quickly, enjoyment is at a peak,
		30	Peak Performance Range you're very creative, innovative, think quickly, and make good decisions.
		20	Motivation sets in; i.e., see people, do some productive activities
		15	Low motivation; activities such as driving to work, reading a book, taking a walk
		10	Awake, but total comfort, very relaxed, contemplating going to bed
		5	Drifting off, about to fall asleep
		0	Total relaxation; asleep; complete absence of anxiety

Figure 8.1. The SUDS Scale

A psychologist named Joseph Wolpe originated the SUDS Scale. He found that the different levels of anxiety and comfort we experience can be assigned relative positions on a scale.

At the bottom of the scale—at the 0 level—Wolpe assigned the state of total relaxation. In most cases, if we were asleep, we would would be at the 0 level.

The SUDS Scale ranges from 0 to 100. When we feel drowsy—as if we're about to fall asleep—we'd be at about the 5 level. When we're awake, experiencing near total comfort, we're at 10. At the 10 level we may be thinking about taking a break and relaxing or even taking a nap. At 15 we're doing activities that require little motivation, such as driving to our offices, filing papers, or maybe even reading a light book.

But then at 20 on the SUDS scale, motivation sets in. In fact the range in which we are likely to begin to feel motivated is between the 20 and 30 level. At this level on the SUDS scale, we probably would feel compelled to see people. We may begin to do productive activities, such as thinking about calls to be made, or planning our day. Perhaps we'll work with our secretaries to schedule some appointments.

It's not all bread and roses at the 15 to 20 level on the SUDS Scale, however. We experience some dissonance because we feel we *should* do certain things. In fact, our motivation level might be such that we would make a couple of phone calls; although the calls would be nonintimidating ones to someone like a business associate. We might even call a client to ask him or her for some advice or to answer a question. This is the level that may coincide with the beginnings of our need to achieve.

PEAK PERFORMANCE LEVELS

According to the psychologist, Dr. Aaron Hemsley, the true level of optimum productivity lies in the area between 30 and 40 on the SUDS Scale. This range is called the *maximum performance level*. When we experience peak performance, we are at this level. Time flows quickly. We truly enjoy what we're doing. We're immersed in whatever we're doing. We become very creative, think quickly, and find ourselves making decisions effectively.

Often at this peak performance level, we're surprised at how well words flow from our mouths. We might find ourselves saying *exactly* the right things. We also find that our minds are sharp. We recall information, even though our memories may not typically be very good.

In fact, to give you an even better example of this peak performance level, when athletes are primed for a sports competition, you can think of them as being at the 30 to 40 level on the SUDS Scale. If you play tennis, you have probably experienced this peak range in the middle of a match. Think of yourself serving a ball. You're ahead 3 games to 2, and you're trying hard to beat the individual on the other side of the net. Your competitive spirits are flaring. You fully lose track of time. You're concentrating totally and absolutely on winning the tennis match. You think very quickly. You react very fast. And you find that your concentration powers are probably at a height you've rarely experienced before.

The same thing may be true of golf. When you're playing, time goes by very quickly. In fact, you may even be surprised to realize that you've been out on the golf course for four hours. It really doesn't feel like it because you're having such a good time.

In fact, if you've ever done any public speaking, you've probably felt the same sort of enthusiasm and excitement. After the first five or ten minutes, when your initial anxiety has gone away, your mind operates very quickly and you become totally unaware of the time that you've spent speaking. The audience could be aware of the hour, but you're having a great time. Ideas flow quickly; you feel excited and enthusiastic. You really are at peak performance.

If we start feeling anxiety, we are up one level to 45 on the scale. At this level, just above peak performance, we start experiencing avoidance bahaviors. We may begin procrastinating. Perhaps we feel disorganized. We may even dread making phone calls. At this level we would probably feel anxiety in asking for referral calls. We may even experience anger. become upset, or feel frustrated at trying to work on a problem or project.

If we experience more severe pain, we are at the 55 level. When we experience psychologically induced, or *psychosomatic*, illness, such as tension headaches, migraines, muscle pain, or soreness, we have reached the 60 level. We may also be unable to concentrate or be easily distracted. At this level, we may find ourselves daydreaming. We also may become depressed or upset.

When we start to face severe problems, we are at the 70, 80, or 90 levels. We may become increasingly anxious, experience an almost phobic type of fear. Things begin to really bother us and give us deep psychological pain. We find ourselves bad-tempered and extremely irritable.

If you ever find yourself in total panic, you have reached the 100 level—the top of the SUDS Scale. Someone in one of my audiences described this 100 level as how you would feel if you're in your car "following a group of a hundred motorcycle-riding, chain-carrying Hell's Angels, when your horn gets stuck."

Rarely do we ever experience such total panic. When we do, it might be in a situation like being stuck in a traffic jam when you have 15 minutes to make a plane flight—the last flight of that day—for an extremely important meeting. Another example might be the experience the bank examiners had when they went in to close the defaulting Penn Square Bank only to find that their baggage was lost, leaving them nothing more to wear during their stay than what they had on. Or reaching the 100 level on the

SUDS Scale may come from winning a trip to Mexico City in a sales contest, only to find out later that you have to win a trip back.

USING ANXIETY FOR MAXIMUM PRODUCTIVITY

If we keep ourselves between the 30 and 40 level of peak performance on the SUDS Scale, even though we experience a small level of stress or anxiety, it works to our great advantage. Any discomfort or anxiety can actually help us.

A slight amount of discomfort will motivate us. We might see it as a challenge. We will feel enthusiastic and excited about what we're doing. Time will flow very quickly and we'll be at peak performance. In this range we will be surprised at how much we can accomplish.

But, if we have too much discomfort, say at any level 45 or above, this will work against us and we'll actually sabotage ourselves. When the fears we discussed—those of rejection, embarrassment, failure, or success—set in, we are at the 45 level or above on the SUDS Scale. The discomfort we feel causes us to use avoidance behaviors that keep us from doing certain activities that cause the painful anxiety these fears give us.

The four fears I discussed, with their chief symptoms—anxiety and depression—only hurt us when they cause our SUDS level to rise to 45 or higher. If we can decrease our anxiety or discomfort, these self-sabotaging fears will have no impact on our business or personal lives. We then can be as successful and as productive as we want to be, without limiting ourselves.

KNOW YOUR SUDS LEVEL

It's very important to be constantly aware of what your SUDS level is. In fact, you should check your level several times a day. Use the scale in figure 8.1 to determine what level you're at.

It may be difficult to remind yourself to check your SUDS level during the day without using a memory jogger. Some good ways to jog your memory are things like placing a note on top of a paperweight which, when you see it, reminds you to check your SUDS level. This note might be read, *"What Is Your SUDS?"*

Another good memory jogger is to put something on the pen you usually write with. Put a rubber band at the top of your pen.

But one of the best methods I've ever heard is to use is clear fingernail polish. You could put a drop of clear fingernail polish on the crystal of your watch. Fingernail polish won't stain the crystal, but will make an enamel finish on the crystal. Whenever you look at the time, you will be reminded to determine where you are on the SUDS Scale.

TOO LOW TO MOTIVATIVE—MOVING ON UP

It is just as bad to be too low on the SUDS Scale as it is to be too high. If you are between 0 and 29 level, for example, you probably don't have enough motivation or stress to bring yourself up to peak performance and peak productivity.

There are, however, a number of good ways to move yourself up on the scale to achieve maximum performance. One of these ways is to listen to motivational speakers and follow through on the methods they give for motivation. However, a common complaint about motivational speakers is that they're full of promise but not very effective—like sipping a teaspoon of water while you're walking across a hot desert. It tastes good, but it doesn't satisfy your thirst for long. Motivational speakers are very entertaining, but, unfortunately, their effect is short-lived.

Another way to move up the scale is to use chemicals. I'm talking about eating candy or drinking coffee or cola with caffeine and sugar. Unfortunately, these are also bad because consuming caffeine artificially stimulates the heart rate and consuming sugar sharply increases blood sugar levels. These substances give you a "high" for about half an hour to 45 minutes. But when the effect wears off, you usually feel lower than you did when you first drank the coffee or soda, or ate the candy.

One of the best ways to move up the scale is to get your heartbeat level up by natural means. This helps the adrenaline system work for you instead of against you. When you do get your heartbeat level up, you will feel that it has a similar effect to caffeine.

One of the best ways to move up on the SUDS Scale to the 30 to 40 level is to engage in a good physical exercise program. Activities like jumping rope, swimming, jogging, or even jumping on one of those new rebounding trampolines will get your heartbeat level up so you can raise your SUDS level to peak productivity.

Unfortunately, it's sometimes difficult to go swimming or jogging in the middle of the day. That's why doing some minor exercise, like walking around your office, is a very good way to bring yourself up the scale. You should also do stretching exercises such as touching your tiptoes or twisting your waist.

I've even heard of psychologists and medical doctors recommending that people get up one hour earlier in the morning and exercise. This not only gets us up the SUDS Scale and gives us a sense of well-being, but it also gives us a nice outlook on the day. Getting up an hour earlier lets us to do things like play tennis or racquetball.

It's interesting to go to tennis or racquetball courts at 6:30 or 7:00 in the morning and see how crowded they are. Apparently many businesspeople have already realized that if they do get a rush of adrenaline through physical exercise in the morning, they will have a much better, more productive day.

If you tend to have a very productive morning but slow down around lunchtime, perhaps finding that your SUDS level decreases to about the 10 level, you might consider doing some activity at noon. Instead of having a heavy lunch, perhaps you could eat a sandwich or an apple on your way to engage in midday recreation. Go play tennis or take a walk in a park. Do something as simple as walking down to a restaurant for lunch instead of driving. Do something to raise your level on the SUDS Scale.

SELF-TALK TO BRING UP THE SUDS

During the day, if you feel yourself losing motivation and thus are slipping down the SUDS scale, one other technique works quite well to bring you back up. This is an activity called *self-talk*. One of the best things you can do for yourself is to affirm yourself. In fact, if you've ever driven alone on the highway late at night and you find yourself starting to fall asleep, one way that you can stay awake is to talk to yourself. Talking to yourself usually increases your SUDS level.

If you start talking back to yourself, you may be in for a psychological shock. But self-talk does often work very well to help us work out problems we may have internalized. When we're able to hear our responses and our thoughts spoken out loud, our own thoughts often sound a little bit ridiculous. Self-talking helps tune us back in to what's really important and what's real in life.

If you don't wish to hold conversations with yourself, perhaps you could give yourself self-motivational affirmations such as, "I'm looking good," or "I'm going to be successful today."

You've probably even heard some people reciting their favorite passage: "Today is the first day of the rest of my life," or, "Every day, I'm getting better and better, and this is going to be my best day ever."

MOVING DOWN THE SUDS SCALE

More important, you also need to know ways to move down the scale. If you're above a 45 level on the SUDS Scale, you're destroying your productivity. Your anxiety is too high. You're causing yourself to dread your work. When your SUDS is high you may use avoidance behaviors like procrastination and disorganization, and you may avoid making necessary phone calls. Anxiety may really control you at this stage.

When you're anxious, your muscles become tense. It's a natural stress response. Too much adrenaline flows through your body; your muscles tense up causing tension headaches. You may also become increasingly upset. But if you can ask your secretary or even an officemate to rub your shoulders for a moment, your tenseness will usually dissipate and you'll also move down the SUDS scale while you're being massaged.

We can eradicate the anxiety brought on by the four self-sabotaging fears by doing something called *progressive relaxation*. It's probably the best way to move down the SUDS Scale—if we're above the 45 level—to the 30 to 40 level of peak performance.

The best time to start using progressive relaxation is in solitude in the evening. Imagine yourself going into a peaceful, wooded forest. Spend approximately 5 minutes imagining yourself walking down into the forest, about 20 minutes in the forest, and 5 minutes to walk out.

Do it by yourself in a quiet room in a very comfortable chair. Loosen your tie or unbutton your top blouse button and relax as much as you can.

Then do this during the day whenever your SUDS level is higher than 45. Take about 90 seconds to 2 minutes. Have your secretary hold your calls. Take about three deep breaths and exhale slowly. Visualize yourself back in the forest for just about one minute, take three more breaths and go back to work. This will indeed drop you right down to the peak performance 30 to 40 level causing you to be more productive than perhaps you have been in years.

I worked with a securities broker recently, who told me that he could usually predict when he was moving above the 45 level on the SUDS Scale. He would start grabbing his pencils more tightly. In fact, he would often break them. He'd feel tense and frustrated much more easily when making phone calls, which would raise his SUDS level even higher. He'd also find himself dreading having to make those calls. I taught him the progressive relaxation technique so that every time he started feeling like he was above the 45 level on the SUDS Scale, he would sit back in his chair, even though he was in a room with ten other salespeople. He would close his eyes for ninety seconds and, after taking three deep breaths, think of himself in that forest. When he opened his eyes again, he was at his peak productivity level where he actually, totally, and absolutely found himself ready, willing, and able to make another phone call. He found rejection had much less effect on him. He experienced much less tension and much more effectiveness in his job.

Obviously, when we experience less anxiety doing highly productive activities that make money for us—like making phone calls or talking to clients we will in turn become much more profitable. In fact, we'll be very surprised at how productive we'll be, and, as a result, the amount of money we will make.

9

Staying in Your Peak Performance Range: How to Beat Call Reluctance

David prides himself on being thorough. He considers himself to be a pro, but he'd like his sales production to be a little higher. He's tired of watching new producers outperform him. *They* really don't know *everything* about their product. He, on the other hand, is *always* prepared and knows *exactly* what to say. The problem is, he doesn't say it often enough. Rather than face his fear of failure, he'd rather spend time analyzing than acting.

Brian considers himself successful. He is image-conscious and knows how to act appropriately. Prospects like to deal with people who have style and class. Brian wants to be nothing short of the very best salesperson around. His self-image affects his behavior. He doesn't prospect much because he feels it is beneath him. To avoid his fear of embarrassment and possible loss of self-perceived status, he dedicates much of his time to industry organizations and professional groups. He rationalizes that networking is better than prospecting. He would rather rely on word-of-mouth to get new clients. Unfortunately, this technique of relying on others to refer prospects to him has never paid off. Brian figures it's at least better than exposing himself to prospects who don't know him.

Patricia enjoys selling. She likes helping people solve their problems. But she realizes that selling, while extremely profitable, can also be uncomfortable. She doesn't like to prospect on referrals or cold calls. She is afraid of being thought of as pushy and intrusive. She frequently apologizes to prospects for interrupting them. She hesitates to pick up the phone and start dialing, waiting for the right time to call. Patricia realizes she doesn't make a lot of calls, but she is unwilling to deal with her fear of rejection, and take the risk of appearing too forward.

IDENTIFYING CALL RELUCTANCE

Do you identify with any of these people? Their self-sabotaging fears have resulted in *call reluctance*.

If you realize your productivity is low or that you are prospecting at low levels, you could have call reluctance. You have goals and the motivation to achieve these goals, but you find it emotionally difficult to get yourself to prospect, and thereby to achieve those goals.

According to research by Shannon and Goodson, detailed in their book *The Psychology of Call Reluctance*, more than 40 percent of salespeople report they have experienced call reluctance to such a degree that it nearly ended their carrers. Most managers recognize that call reluctance is the main reason new salespeople frequently fail, but few comprehend the impact it can have on more experienced producers, causing them to become complacent about prospecting calls.

A financial planner, who has been in the business for more than ten years, wrote me recently. I am on friendly terms with him since we see each other every week at our church Sunday School class. He knows me well enough to call by phone, but instead he sent me a four-page boiler plate prospecting letter. It must have taken him at least an hour to dictate, not to mention the time his secretary took to type it. The letter described his company's background as well as his recommendations concerning my personal finances. It was so impersonal, I erased my name and scratched in "Dear Occupant," then showed it to my wife. She thought it was a joke, and we promptly tossed it into the trash. A standard, impersonal letter may work as a cold entry, but it indicated that my financial planner friend was experiencing call reluctance.

TYPES OF CALL RELUCTANCE

The first step in dealing with call reluctance is to recognize specifically what it is and how it is affecting you. While there are numerous character types who experience call reluctance, four stand out as the most common

Analytic
Image-conscious
Position-acceptance
Fear-of-intrusion

The Analyzing Reluctant

Analytic call reluctance occurs in salespeople who are overly concerned about being swept away by their emotions. Afraid to show their true feelings, they preoccupy themselves in highly technical matters. Analytics keep their feelings in the deep freeze. They are afraid to reveal themselves because they suffer from the fear of rejection.

They overanalyze and underact, appearing reserved and self-restrained in interpersonal conversations. When they give sales presentations, they tend to stress information while neglecting emotions. They sometimes even seem cynical about the value of interpersonal relations and people skills.

92

When I was a stockbroker, I knew an analytic type, named Frank. Frank had been with the firm for about five years and was very knowledgeable. In between my daily load of 150-plus cold calls, I would pop into his office for inspiration and advice. Each time I saw him, he was looking over a stock performance history or working on one of his computer-based stock illustrations. I was shocked to learn that out of the 15 or so producers in our company, he was in the bottom 25 percent.

The Image-Conscious Type

The image-conscious type of call reluctance is prevalent in salespeople who try to overcome self-confidence and self-esteem insecurities by making a show of the trappings of success. These people commonly suffer from fear of failure and often fear of success as well. They invest heavily in the appearance of wealth and achievement.

Ostentatious in their displays of success, this type maintains a constant vigilance against any threat to their advertised respect and net worth. In an effort to impress others, they often work on showy if not difficult cases. Lacking qualifications or experience, they nevertheless spend time working on big endeavors with a low probability of success, believing these infrequent "hot" deals are compatible with their perceived professional image. Prospecting is beneath them and is seen as just plain undignified.

An insurance agent I know fits this mold. He wears so much gold jewelry he looks like an executive Mr. T. He often employs others to make cold calls for him, due to what he says is his lack of time. His production is low because he is still "streamlining his operation." He has a condescending way of speaking softly that makes others uncomfortable. You get the feeling that he sells a few large cases per year (which he brags about), although his profit margin is barely enough to support his financial needs. He continues to avoid prospecting until he's financially forced back into it to create more business.

Position-Acceptance Type

The position-acceptance type of call reluctance occurs when salespeople suffer from fear of embarrassment. They are embarrassed or apologetic in their role as salesperson. They often suppress their sense of dedication and zeal because they don't believe their job or position is professionally impressive. They sense they are a disappointment to some significant person in their lives.

Position-acceptance types may suffer from periods of job-related depression. While pretending to be committed, they never fully believe the job will become a career. They may not believe that sales, or at least the type of sales they do, is valid or worthwhile.

I speak frequently to insurance organizations populated by CPAs, CFPs, MBAs, or others who feel sales is not a career for those with "smarts." Recently a new insurance agent showed me his card. Linked with a major life insurance company, he had been in the field only about 18 months. Instead of saying "Insurance Agent," the card introduced him as "Leigh Smith, Financial Consultant."

I asked him if he sold securities. He said, "Not really. I actually sell insurance products."

He probably had no idea that he was exhibiting classic signs of suffering from the position-acceptance type of call reluctance.

Fear-of-Intrusion Type

Fear-of-Intrusion types don't want to be considered pushy or too aggressive. They frequently suffer from fear of embarrassment.

Fear-of-intrusion types are unwilling to be assertive in prospecting for new business. They frequently lose control of the conversation or appointment, demonstrating an unwillingness to keep the prospect focused on the purpose of their call—that is, when they do actually prospect. They are overly concerned about the needs and desires of other people.

A fear-of-intrusion type of salesperson may postpone making a prospecting call because he or she is waiting for the right time to call or for an assurance that the prospect really wants to talk with him or her. Unfortunately, the salesperson is rarely able to find this "right" time, "right" person, and "right" place. Fear-of-intrusion types *might* make a call on a qualified referral but are very reluctant to call on prospects.

These people frequently accept a prospect's objections too quickly and have trouble closing a sale. They may view highly aggressive salespeople as unprofessional. While they are warm and sociable, they often let the needs of others take precedence over their own objectives.

I spent a few hours with a new salesperson, observing her prospecting skills. She was excited about dealing with people on the telephone but was a little intimidated by gruff prospects. I listened to her approach. She said, "Hi, Mr. Prospect. My name is Alana Berg. I'm with Prime Investment Company. Did I interrupt anything? Were you busy? If so, I could call back later."

That's all l needed to hear. I quickly zeroed in on her lack of assertiveness. She said she had trouble believing that what she wanted to talk about was as important as what the prospect was doing when she called. She clearly suffered from the fear-of-intrusion type of call reluctance.

DEALING WITH CALL RELUCTANCE

Albert Ellis, PhD, a leader in *rational emotive therapy*, has an interesting way of dealing with phobics. He believes that we engage in a series of irrational thoughts to support a fear—whether it is a fear of heights, a fear of asking a prospect to buy a product or service, or any of the four self-sabotaging fears that limit our productivity.

These irrational mental processes reinforce our own negative self-image. For example, a salesperson might pick up a telephone and internally worry, "This prospect really isn't a very good referral. I've dealt with this type of person before. They're rude and curt. I really don't think now is a good time to call. Executives like this always get lots of calls in the morning from salespeople. I think I'll wait until the afternoon when things slow down for him."

Ellis believes that if we can interrupt and replace such internal dialogues of irrational thought patterns, we can allow ourselves to lose this "extra baggage" we carry.

4 EASY STEPS TO GETTING RID OF CALL RELUCTANCE

Use these four steps the next time you have a bout of call reluctance

1. Observe
2. Pattern-Interrupt
3. Substitute
4. Reward

Observe

First, observe yourself experiencing call reluctance. Pay careful attention to what you are going through. Chances are you have let your self-sabotaging irrational thoughts drag your personal esteem through the mud. As you did with Bandler's and Grinder's "3-Minute Phobia Cure" in chapter 7, you should try detaching yourself from your thoughts and behavior. Simply be an observer instead of a participant.

An insurance agent recently tested this method. Just as he was about to make a call to a referral lead, he started feeling the call reluctance panic. His palms became moist and his heart palpitated. He also became aware of his mental irrational dialogue: "I really don't want to make this call. I feel myself becoming afraid of the telephone. If the prospect thinks I am intruding on his time, what will I say? He won't think I warrant any of his time because he'll know I'm new at this type of call. He'll probably recognize how scared I am of talking with him." The insurance agent observed how his fears were influencing his logical thought.

Pattern-Interrupt

The second step is to interrupt the destructive behavior pattern. By recognizing when the irrational thought patterns of call reluctance are setting in, we can interrupt ourselves. Irrational thoughts seem to feed on themselves in a compounding way, like a snowball increasing in size rolling down a snowy hill.

Next time you observe that call reluctance patterns have surfaced, immediately do something physical. Stand up and walk around your office. Say out loud what you are thinking.

One of the best ways to interrupt the pattern is to cause yourself quick physical discomfort. Wear a rubber band around your wrist, and when you become self-sabotaging, snap the rubber band. The sting will break the cycle.

Substitute

Third, immediately substitute a positive experience to replace a negative one. If you have been selling for even a few weeks, you have probably made a successful phone call. Recall how easy that call was and how good you felt during and after the conversation. Get a 3 x 5 file card, write down that name, and record every detail of how you felt during and after that call.

Reward

And finally, after every call, give yourself an immediate reward.

Whether you were able to speak to your prospect or not, reward yourself.

A reward can be anything from a sip of coffee to calling your spouse—or even popping a breath mint into your mouth. The reward reinforces the phone call and increases the likelihood that you will make another call.

A financial planner with the fear of intrusion recently used this four-step technique. He realized he felt almost apologetic for even making a phone call. His heart palpitated and sweat beaded on his forehead before his calls. Then he observed his own phobic reaction, interrupted himself with a rubberband snap, substituted with a memory of a successful call, and drank a cup of coffee as a reward after he made the call. Not only did his level of anxiety decrease, he finally was able to increase his revenues on the telephone and also to call past referrals for appointments he had put off for months.

If you are good on the phone, you'll be light-years ahead of your competition. Your productivity will increase. When you can learn to recognize how the four self-sabotaging fears can cause call reluctance, and you can identify the type of call reluctance you have, then you can do something about it. When you do, business will simply flow to you.

10

Setting Objectives

You now have information that can enable you to

Recognize the psychological barriers to productivity
Monitor your level of psychological discomfort
Overcome the anxiety your fears bring

Now you can begin to build a tailor-made productivity program through which you can achieve your objectives.

DECIDING WHAT YOUR OBJECTIVES ARE

First, we being with goals and goal-setting.
Webster's *New Collegiate Dictionary* defines *goal* as

"the terminal point of a race."

This is really the focus of *Peak Performance Selling: How to Increase Your Sales by 70% in 6 Weeks*—to help you accomplish your race toward a goal, whether it is to lose weight, modify your child's behavior, own your dream car or house, or make your company the most profitable ever in its industry. We want you to get your goals.

DECIDING WHAT YOU WANT

Consider some examples of goals other people have set. If you have already set your own goals, don't tune out. The theory and methodology may help you refine your already set goals into more workable ones.

Relax. We are not going to go into great detail about why you need to have goals or how to set goals. In fact, we assume you have already set at least one or several goals and are looking for a way to achieve them. If you haven't, you can easily come up with something you would like to have. Think of something you've always wanted.

To build your tailor-made productivity program, it is crucial that you have *some* basis for your goals as the first step in this goal-getting system.

A few years ago, a friend of mine named Ty Boyd, a talk show host on a local television station in North Carolina, was busy looking for people to interview. He found out that H. L. Hunt, the billionaire who with only a fifth-grade education made his fortunes in oil and ketchup, was going to be in the North Carolina area. Boyd promptly sent a letter to Hunt asking if he would be on the show. Hunt replied that he would love to, but, because of his schedule, he could not for six months.

The time went by very slowly as Ty kept thinking about Hunt, the man who won his first oil well in a game of five-card stud. Hunt swapped the well for oil leases and then struck a hard bargain with a legendary wildcatter named Columbus "Dad" Joiner. Hunt then gained control of a vast oil field in East Texas. At one point it was rumored that Hunt had personally earned $1 million in one week—and that was in 1943!

Finally, Hunt appeared on the program. After fifteen to twenty minutes of chatting with Hunt about the economy and his favorite investments, Boyd asked him a question he had been waiting months to ask. He asked, "How did you become so successful so fast?"

As Hunt paused for the answer, Ty Boyd remembered concentrating so hard on what Hunt was about to say that he forgot about the studio audience—all he could think about was the information that would change his life totally. But the reply was so obvious that it startled Ty Boyd.

Hunt said simply, "Decide what you want."

"Decide what you want," is all Hunt said. Simple, yes? But this thought helped Hunt become as wealthy as anyone could be in this country. Hunt went on to say one other thing, however, "Decide what you want, but also decide what you'll do to get it."

It's easy to desire things. But are we really prepared to make the sacrifice, to work hard for what we want? There are no magical pathways, no fast freeways to getting the things we desire. We must make a decision about what we *really* want, otherwise we'll flounder like a ship with no rudder. A friend of mine once observed that most people are waiting for their ship to come in, but unfortunately they're waiting at the bus depot.

SET OBJECTIVES—KNOW WHAT RACE YOU'RE RUNNING

Unless you want to drift through life, undirected like a helium-filled balloon set free, *you must set goals*. Set objectives, otherwise you'll never know exactly what you're working toward or what race you're running.

Look at figures 10.1 through 10.4, titled "Objectives." Study figures 10.1–10.3, then, using the blank objective sheet in figure 10.4 as a model, please write, in the spaces provided, the goals you want to achieve in the

OBJECTIVES

OBJECTIVE	COST	WHEN
1 380 SL Mercedes	$52,000	12/88
2 Midsummer vacation in Europe	$ 5,000	6/88
3 New rental property	$80,000	3/89
4 Achieve top sales of year award	$150,000 commissions	12/88
5 Achieve sales quality award	Extra education courses 6/89	
6		

HOW ATTAINED By making more sales.

Current activity level: 2 phone calls/day = 1 booked appointment every 2 days = 1 appointment every week = 1 sale every 2 weeks. Current averages: 1 sale = $250 commission = 2 appointments = 5 booked appointments = 20 calls.

Extra activity needed to achieve objectives by date desired: 10 calls/day = 2 booked appointments/day = 1 appointment/day = 1 sale every 2 days = 2 sales/week = $2000/month ($1500 more than I'm making now!!!!)

Figure 10.1. Objectives

next one, three, and five years. Make sure these are goals you truly want— goals you are willing to work for.

The goals you list should be specific and tangible. They must be achievements for which you can chart a plan. They should also be measurable. Goals such as "being happy" are important and nice but are not specific enough for this sales performance program.

The objective "To make more money" is not specific at all. If you want to make $50,000 more per year, *that* is specific. If you want to write, "I want to be happy," then specify exactly what would make you happy. If doing business in a new market would make you happier, then write in a specific target number of sales you want to achieve in that market. If starting a new company would make you happier, write that in, too.

Make sure you specify exactly what you want in the next one, three, and five years. These are your short-, medium-, and long-term goals.

OBJECTIVES

OBJECTIVE	COST	WHEN
1 Read 1 book/week	1/2 hour/night	within 30 days
2		
3		
4		
5		
6		

HOW ATTAINED By using reward system and reading for
30 minutes every evening, so my level of reading activity
slowly goes up to 1 book/week.

Figure 10.2. Objectives

OBJECTIVES

OBJECTIVE	COST	WHEN
1 To control child's messiness	30 minutes/day	by 30 days
2		
3		
4		
5		
6		

HOW ATTAINED By rewarding child's neatness and
staying on contract until end of program.
Also, by abiding by the terms of the contract.

Figure 10.3. Objectives

There are two basic types of goals

1. Business or financial goals
2. Personal goals (i.e., What do you want for your family or for yourself in the next one, three, and five years?)

Be sure to include both types of goals on your objectives list.

When you have completed your objectives list, place it in a spiral notebook or a folder. Use this as your peak performance workbook.

VISUALIZE YOUR GOALS

The second step in building your goal-setting productivity program is called *visualizing your goals*. Remember how when we were children we all used pictures to reinforce our goals or the things we wanted to achieve? In fact, young children or teenagers often put on their bedroom walls posters or photos of people they look up to as heroes

Superman

Wonder Woman

He-Man of the Universe or She-Ra

Later on, pictures of music and rock stars or even sports heroes find their place on children's walls.

As adults, we can use the same technique to accomplish and achieve the objectives we want. Usually we try to remember goals in our minds. They are quickly forgotten, however, because we don't have physical reminders, like those posters of heroes, that serve to remind us of what we want.

We need to do the same thing we did when we were children: *Put a picture or a poster up in your office or on the bathroom mirror.* An equally good method is to use a picture or an advertisement from a magazine that depicts exactly what we want.

But we like to think that we are more sophisticated than children— that we don't need to use a child's tricks to remind us of what we want. Let's look at an inspirational winner from the sports world from whom we can learn a lot about goals and see how he used this "child's trick" to become the "World's Greatest Athlete."

Most people remember that in the 1976 Olympics, Bruce Jenner won a gold medal for the decathlon. He defeated both the Russian and East German star decathletes. But most people do not recall that in 1972, Bruce

<u>OBJECTIVES</u>

OBJECTIVE	COST	WHEN
1		
2		
3		
4		
5		
6		

HOW ATTAINED

Figure 10.4. Objectives

Jenner was also in the Olympics in Munich. In Munich, Germany, Jenner placed 10th in the decathlon. Heartbroken, he decided he would do something to improve his performance and also keep his ambition and motivation at a peak.

In 1972, Jenner saw a newspaper article depicting that year's Olympic winners. The article heralded the greatness of the 1972 decathlon winner, Russian Nikolai Avilov, who had scored more points in the decathlon than any previous decathlete. Jenner cut the article out of the newspaper and put his own picture over the photo of Avilov. He also wrote in the distances and race times that he wanted to achieve in each event in 1976 when he was determined to go back to the Olympics and try again for the decathlon gold medal.

In his apartment in California, Jenner put the newspaper clipping with his picture, the distances, and the race times on his bathroom mirror so that he would look at it every day. He knew that if he committed it to memory by seeing it every day, he would achieve his goal four years later.

Jenner not only was able to achieve his goal of winning the decathlon gold medal, but he also was able to surpass every distance and time that he visualized he could achieve. He surpassed all expectations, scoring a greater number of points than anyone before in the Olympic decathlon event. Every day he had been reminded by the picture to visually reinforce himself and give himself a motivational charge.

Look at figures 10.5 and 10.6, titled "Visualized Objectives." Using figure 10.6 as your model, make your own visualized objective sheet. Look at figure 10.5 to see how someone used the visualized objective sheet to reach the objective of getting a BMW 635 CSI.

To your visualized objective sheet, attach a photo or a magazine clipping showing the objects you want to try to get within the next one, three, and five years. Put that photo or clipping in the space provided.

Below it write down what it is, how much it costs, when you want it, and what you'll have to do to get it.

Put a copy of the visualized objective sheet you've created in the front of the folder or notebook you are using as your productivity workbook so that every time you look at the workbook, you'll have to look at the pictures of the things you want to achieve. This will help improve your overall attitude about working hard to get the things you want. It will also help you to keep clearly in mind exactly what you're working for.

VISUALIZED OBJECTIVE

OBJECTIVE ___BMW 635 CSI_____

COST ___$52,000_____

WHEN DO YOU WANT IT? ___DECEMBER/1988_____

WHAT WILL YOU DO TO GET IT?___SELL 2 PRODUCTS____

PER WEEK AT AVERAGE COMMISSION OF $250 EACH.

Figure 10.5. Visualized Objective

VISUALIZED OBJECTIVE

PLACE
PHOTO
HERE

OBJECTIVE _____

COST _____

WHEN DO YOU WANT IT? _____

WHAT WILL YOU DO TO GET IT? _____

_____

_____

_____

_____

Figure 10.6. Visualized Objective

11

Game Planning: Applying the Goal to Averages

Goals are tremendous, but they mean absolutely nothing if we don't know how hard we have to work to get them. It's like starting a race without knowing the course, the distance to be covered, or what the time or speed expectations are.

To achieve any goal, we first need to know about how much effort we need to expend to get that goal—to acquire it. Most people set a goal without understanding what they have to do to get it. All too often, they aren't prepared for the effort or cost they must expend in achieving a goal.

Anyone can have a goal. Few people achieve their goal, however, unless they know specifically what they want and how hard they are willing to work to get it.

Based on the information in this chapter, you can design a basic plan which can help you plot out exactly how much work you will have to do to achieve whatever objective you have in mind.

THE 3-POINT BASIC OBJECTIVE SETTING PLAN

1. Figure the Cost of the Goal?

Number one, figure out first how much your goal costs in terms of dollars, time, or, in the case of weight loss, pounds. If your objective is a five-bedroom house, how much does it cost? What are you willing to put down as a deposit, and how large a mortgage payment are you willing to make?

If you want to lose weight and feel that membership in a health spa or gym is necessary, write down the cost. You should also decide how much time every day you are willing to spend exercising at the spa.

2. Decide When You Want Your Goal

Number two, decide when you want your goal. Specify the year and even the month as closely as possible.

When do you want your dream house? "As soon as possible" is too vague. Mark down a month. What month are you prepared to successfully end your diet? Or what month do you want to complete that fence you've been thinking about?

3. What Must You Do to Achieve Your Goal

Number three, determine what you need to do to achieve your goal. You know it's probably not filing paperwork which would help you acquire that objective. More likely, it's selling more products.

Decide exactly what you need to do to achieve your goal by the date you want it. What activity will help give you your objective? Prospecting in a new market? Or just plain seeing more clients?

If your objective is being more efficient in the morning, your activity might be getting to work a half-hour earlier. Or writing a "things to do" list the first fifteen minutes in your office.

Use the "3-Point Basic Objective Setting Plan" to

1. Figure the Cost of Your Goal
2. Decide When You Want Your Goal
3. Decide What Must You Do to Achieve Your Goal

If you use it right away, it will help you become organized in setting up your sales performance program. It will help you reach your objectives.

Now you have set your goal, and you know how much it costs, exactly when you want it, and what activities you need to do to get it.

For example, if your objective is a 380 SL Mercedes,

1. How many more sales per month do you need to make to acquire that Mercedes when you want it?
2. How many more face-to-face appointments must you go on during the month to make the additional sales?
3. How many more appointments must you book during the day, week, and month to achieve that goal?
4. How many more phone calls must you make during the day, week, and month to achieve that goal?

CHARTING YOUR CURRENT ACTIVITY

To get an idea of how hard you are currently working, refer to figure 11.1, "What Are Your Averages?" and figure 11.2, "Current Activity."

Use figure 11.1 to figure out how many booked appointments and sales calls you actually end up going on to get one sale. For example, one sale for you may require 40 calls, which result in four booked appoint-

---

WHAT ARE YOUR AVERAGES?

1 SALE = _____ # APPTS = _____ # BOOKED APPTS = _____ # CALLS

OR 1 SALE = WHAT TARGET ACTIVITY

FOR EXAMPLE: 1 SALE = 3 APPTS = 4 BOOKED APPTS = 40 CALLS
               1 SALE = 40 CALLS
     IF   1 SALE = $800 COMMISSION, THEN 1 CALL = $20

Figure 11.1. What Are Your Averages?

ments, or three appointments. If you get an $800 commission for each sale, then one call would be worth $20 to you.

Using figure 11.2, you can determine whether or not your current activity is helping you achieve your goal.

These figures can be used for sales behaviors or any other target behaviors you would like to reach.

Use figures 11.3 to 11.6 as models for charting your current activity. If your target behavior is to make more sales, your graph may look like figure 11.3, where phone calls equal a straight line, booked appointments a broken line, and sales a dotted line. Figure 11.4 shows a similar graph with reading as the target behavior. Figure 11.5 charts a child's good behavior as the target.

CURRENT ACTIVITY

What are you currently doing each day and week to get your goal?

Sales/week or day _____   # Appts/week or day _____

Booked appts/week or day _____   # Calls/week or day _____

OTHER TARGET BEHAVIORS
1. Tardiness: How often are you late (or on time)?
2. Reading: How many pages are you currently reading each day/week?
3. How often does your child misbehave? How often does your child follow instructions?
4. How many pounds do you want to lose?

Figure 11.2. Current Activity

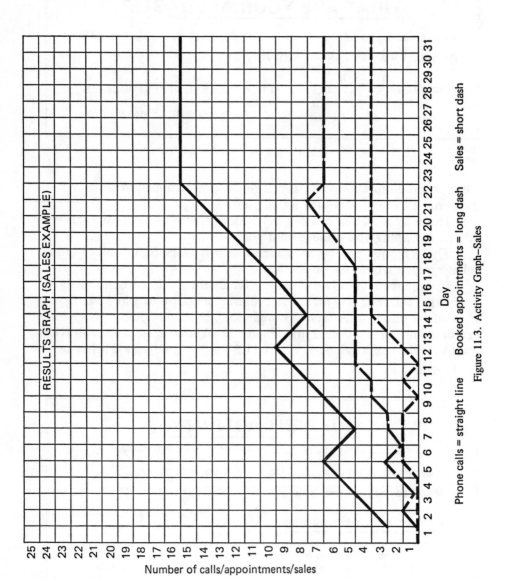

Figure 11.3. Activity Graph–Sales

Phone calls = straight line   Booked appointments = long dash   Sales = short dash

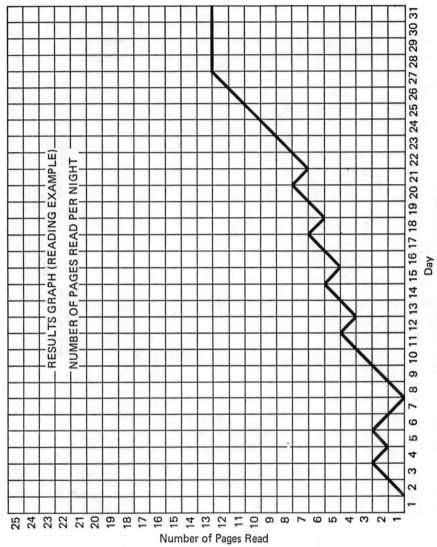

Figure 11.4. Activity Graph–Reading

117

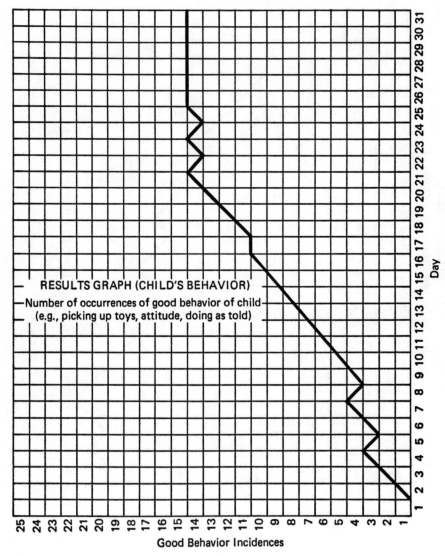

RESULTS GRAPH (CHILD'S BEHAVIOR)

Number of occurrences of good behavior of child (e.g., picking up toys, attitude, doing as told)

Good Behavior Incidences

Day

Figure 11.5. Activity Graph–Child's Behavior

118

CURRENT ACTIVITY GRAPH

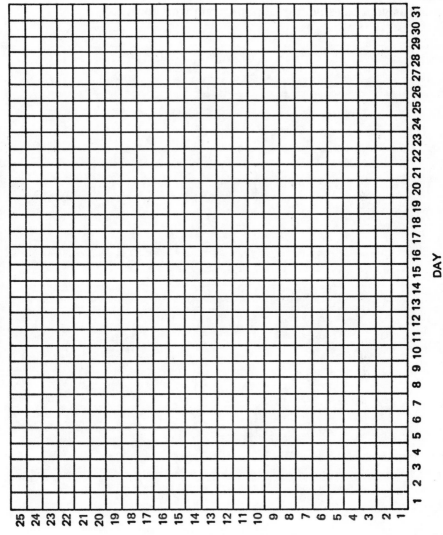

Figure 11.6. Current Activity Graph

119

Game Planning: Applying the Goal to Averages

Working through how you'll perform your activity when you set the objective will give you a good idea of how hard you'll have to work for it, compared to your current level of productivity. Keep a copy of your averages and your current activity graph in the notebook or folder you are using as your sales performance program workbook.

12

Building Your Averages: Your Immediate and Deferred Reward Systems

One of the only ways we can achieve a goal is to know our habit patterns and performance averages—or our present *modus operandi*.

When we have a handle on how we spend our time and how much effort we are expending, we may be very surprised.

KNOWING YOUR AVERAGES

Many of us fall into ruts. Day after day, we start to fall into habits of doing things that are very nonproductive. We take on behaviors that cause us to avoid activities we need to do—activities that would help us perform more efficiently and effectively.

You should ask yourself the following questions once a month, if not once a week, because knowing your current activity level and production averages (see figures 11.1 and 11.2) is essential to being productive:

What are our current levels of activity?

How much are we doing right now to get what we want?

How much work are we doing to get our job done?

What are we doing right now to make more money?

Or ask these questions:

What are we doing now to lose that excess weight?

What methods are we using to discipline our children?

How is our time spent trying to achieve our goals?

You can never hope to succeed unless you know exactly how you spend your time.

I recently talked to a very depressed new salesperson who hated to call prospects. After interviewing him for a few hours, I finally found out how he was spending his time and what his averages were. I found that his averages were very poor. In fact, out of every 20 calls he made, he would only get one appointment. Normally for his type of business it took ten calls to get an appointment.

But even though his averages were poor, he discovered that for each phone call, based on the commission he was receiving, he made roughly

$3. In other words, for every twenty calls he made he would schedule an appointment which down the line would give him one sale, so that for every twenty calls he was making approximately $60.

Think of how much more motivating it is to make those calls knowing each one yields $3. Instead of viewing the nonproductive calls as rejections or as worthless, each call—results or not—is worthwhile.

If you're in sales or management, you probably already know that if you put in a high degree of effort and activity you will profit from your labors. You reap what you sow.

In the previous example, if the salesman wanted to increase his income by $20 each day, he would have to make seven additional phone calls every day. At this rate, according to his averages, at the end of the month, allowing for twenty-two working days, he should experience a gain in income of $462 as a result of the extra sales his activity would yield.

If you're a salesperson, is your phone call worth $3? Is it worth $10? Or $15? Is seeing a prospect or seeing a client worth $15? Or is it worth $100?

Sometimes when we know exactly how much value there is in a given activity, we find much greater motivation to do the activity.

A couple of years ago, I worked as a consultant for a Fortune 500 computer company. We worked with the salespeople and sales managers. In our research, we determined that the salespeople were being financially rewarded for making sales, but not rewarded for all the activity leading up to the sales.

The company agreed to an experiment which I directed. We slightly decreased sales commissions and instead gave the salespeople $5 for every phone call they made prospecting for new business. As expected, phone calls increased dramatically, which also increased appointments, which in turn led to increased sales and commissions.

4-POINT INDEX TO AVERAGES

Take a sheet of paper and figure out your averages. Use figure 11.1 as a guideline.

1. Start with the initial activity, whether it is making a phone call, jogging, or diet control. If you are a salesperson making a sale, how many appointments does it take before you make a sale? Please write that down.

2. How many appointments do you book before you actually complete one? When you book an appointment, sometimes you have "fall-out"—people who call you up and say they can't make it. On the average, how many appointments do you need to book to go on a face-to-face interview or physical appointment?

3. How many telephone calls do you make before getting a booked appointment? These telephone calls can be referrals or cold calls. How many of these phone calls do you make to get one booked appointment? Or perhaps, how many doors do you need to knock on before you talk to someone?

Please record these numbers. By doing so, you should have a good idea of exactly how much activity is needed to get one sale.

When we see how much activity we must invest to make one sale—how many appointments we need to go on, how many phone calls we need to make—or, in weight loss, how many sodas not to indulge in, we are usually very surprised.

4. I would like you to calculate the amount of money you could make for each telephone call you complete before making a sale. I'd also like you to calculate the amount of money you make on each appointment you complete before making a sale.

Many times this simple exercise of calculating the amount of money we can make at each step of the process, rather than calculating only the amount of money per sale, serves as a very nice motivational lift to help you feel better about the work you are doing right now.

Keep the "4-Point Index to Averages" handy, perhaps on an index card in your purse or wallet, inside your office drawer, or posted near the phone so that each time you begin to experience a drop in motivation you can remind yourself that each call has a dollar value, and some simple multiplication can easily motivate you to get going. If you don't know for sure what your averages are, take a typical week and record very accurately your daily activities. Remember to keep track of the following

1. How many appointments you go on before making a sale.

2. How many appointments you book before completing one.

3. How many telephone calls you need to make to get one booked sale.

4. The amount of money you could make per phone call or appointment completed before making a sale.

If you are applying this to non-sales goals, record other activities you are doing right that will help you achieve your objective.

I recently worked with an insurance agent who worked for a major firm. His name is Craig. Craig wanted a 633 CSi BMW. Craig's average commission on a sale was approximately $500. He knew that to lease this BMW would cost around $450 a month. Craig also knew that one sale equalled two closing interviews, which also equalled about five opening interviews or face-to-face appointments, which in turn equalled five booked appointments since he had no fallout, which equalled approximately 20 referral calls.

Craig realized he needed to increase his activity by $450 every month to pay for this new BMW. This translated into making four extra phone calls, one extra booked appointment, and one face-to-face opening appointment per week, which in turn translated to one closing interview every two weeks and approximately one sale every month, which equalled about $500.

Craig was easily able to find out exactly how much effort and work he needed to do to acquire that BMW exactly when he wanted it.

LESS TANGIBLE GOALS

Whenever effort expended is laid out in this manner, with a definite work plan, goals not only seem within reach, but they also seem almost *easy* to reach. But perhaps your goal is not a physical object, like a BMW.

Maybe your goal is something less tangible, like gaining more knowledge about your business. Obviously gaining more knowledge in itself is not a goal. Specifying precisely what you want to know is a goal. Maybe it's more product knowledge you want. But you must be even more specific, such as deciding you want to learn about new taxation policies. And be even more specific: decide to learn exactly which taxation benefits help your business most in selling your product.

You probably have a good idea how many hours of extra reading you need to do weekly or daily to achieve the level of competency or knowledgeability about your business. You'll need to specify how many seminars or conferences you plan to attend and by when you want to achieve your goal of becoming more knowledgeable.

You need to decide how much effort you must and will put in over and above your present levels to achieve the goal or objective that you want when you want it.

WHERE IS YOUR EFFORT GOING? THE 80/20 RULE

If you are a manager or a salesperson who would like to do more to help yourself become more productive without using averages, you need to determine where your effort is going.

The "80/20 Rule" says that, in most cases, 80 percent of our effort results in 20 percent of our productivity. Is this true with you? Is 20 percent of your business growth taking 80 percent of your time?

The "80/20 Rule" is a very old-line management concept, which leads many industrial psychologists to believe that most people in business are not spending their time and effort effectively. People are not as efficient as they could be in doing the things that make them the most money.

If you're a manager, what I'd like you to do is think about the activity or program that yields you the highest business return on investment. I'd also like you to think about what you have to do to increase your income.

If you're a manager with a set salary and no extra income source(s), such as a commission, what do you have to do to increase your income by bonuses, by overrides, or even by promotions?

Do you need to hire one salesperson a month?

Do you need to terminate other salespeople?

Do you need to hold more meetings?

Do you need more training and development sessions?

Do you simply need to use better time management techniques?

Exactly what do you need to do to make yourself more efficient in your business?

I have worked with a number of managers. I recall one in particular, who was hard working and had a tremendous talent for his type of management of salespeople. But he complained about not having enough time to do the things he needed to do.

This is a very typical management complaint. This manager knew he needed to develop new marketing plans but found he spent more than six hours a day solving his salespeople's problems and doing paperwork. He felt guilty and upset that he couldn't accomplish things he knew he had to accomplish, and he also found he had to work more than twelve hours a day to try to make up for the time he spent solving problems.

WHAT'S YOUR ACTIVITY LEVEL?

The overall message here is to get you to determine

What are you trying to accomplish in your business?
What steps do you need to take to get where you want to be?

Besides knowing what your averages are, besides knowing how much you have to work to achieve a sale or another objective, you also need to know some other *extremely* important information:

What is your activity level right now?
What are you spending your time doing?
Do you know how you are spending your day?

KEEPING A DIARY AND A JOURNAL

A very good way to find out how you're spending your day is to use a diary. In this diary, you should write down every project you do. You should also write down the number of minutes or hours you spend on it. You want to record how much effort you currently expend on each project.

This exercise may prove very embarrassing, since most of us spend too much time doing nonproductive things like chatting with office partners or talking on the phone about personal concerns without realizing that it's taking a big chunk out of our productive day.

By keeping this diary you can learn

On the average day, how many calls you make.
How many people you see or interview.
How many sales you make during the average week.

In addition to the diary, keeping a day-to-day journal is another very important facet of increasing your productivity level. Unlike your diary, in which you list specific activities you've done during the day, your journal is the place for you to write at least one to two paragraphs about your day and thus clearly think through the problems you may encounter as you struggle to change your behavior to achieve more productivity.

Writing about your day in the journal helps you think out on paper the reasons why you want to change and also the good things that happen to you during the day. It gives you a daily outlet for your responses to the rewards and punishments you give yourself, and it also gives you a chance to look back on previous days and recall how you felt. You can compare your days and see how much you're changing—and how much better you feel about the target behaviors you're trying to change.

Journal writing is something psychologists frequently use in therapy. They usually feel that if a client writes down his or her thoughts and feelings, the client will become more introspective and think more about his or her emotions.

If you've ever done any letter writing, even though you don't like to write letters, often you find it's kind of fun, because you're able to concentrate deeply on your own emotional aspects of the things you are writing about. But more important, it brings back a lot of memories, and gives you a chance to think about feelings you usually don't have the time to concentrate on.

Please keep up a daily journal. Try to write at least one paragraph every day you are on this sales performance program.

With the diary—in which you record specific activities—you should try to calculate how much activity you're spending on making calls, seeing or interviewing people, and making sales during the day and during the week.

Use the diary to mark down the number of hours you are doing something or to indicate when you start and when you finish an activity. Above all else, be as honest as possible. Don't try to inflate your activity levels. If you do, you could become frustrated and discouraged.

USING THE DIARY TO KNOW HOW HARD YOU ARE WORKING

What you are trying to find out here, basically, is how hard you are currently working.

What are you spending your time doing?
What benefits is this activity giving you in terms of results?

From research over the past five to ten years, we've found that goals are great, but if you don't know how hard you'll have to work for them, they're meaningless. People who write down a goal expect to achieve it. But when it comes time to actually work for that goal, all of the joy is taken out of it. All the great hopes and ambitions dissipate when people finally realize that having a goal means nothing more than just having a direction on which to focus your effort.

THE SECRET IS WORK

Recently, I was in the offices of the Equitable Life Insurance Company of Iowa. While a manager and I were in his office discussing a project, he took out a varnished block of wood with hinges. On top it said, "The Secret to Success." I opened it to find this secret spelled out:

"W-O-R-K."

Work. Many people, when they find out they have to work hard to achieve their goals decide that having objectives isn't really that wonderful at all. There's no mystery. There's no secret formula to being successful and getting the things you want. Success comes to those who are willing to work for it. And, perhaps even more important, you need to know how hard you'll have to work to achieve the goal.

KNOWLEDGE + A PLAN = RESULTS

The next step is to lay a plan for achieving your goal, based on your own present work habits, and calculate what extra work you need to do to accomplish what you want.

Let me give you an example of how this works.

In the late 1970s I had the great chance to play the top-ranked male tennis player in the world, Guillermo Vilas. Vilas, at that time, had won approximately forty-eight consecutive tennis matches.

Guillermo Vilas was really a killer on the court. He would put away practically every shot, never letting his opponent get more than just a couple of points per game. A real pro, he always went for the jugular every chance he could. After an hour and a half of doubles play, Vilas and his partner won the match. They also went on to win the tournament.

After our doubles match, Vilas and his partner left and my partner and I went back to the clubhouse to change. As we were leaving the tennis stadium, we happened upon a little sidewalk cafe where we spotted Vilas sitting with his coach, a Rumanian named Jan Tiriac.

Tiriac was Vilas' motivational dynamo. A Rumanian with a Fu Manchu moustache, Tiriac was the type of guy who was a real driver, a hardhitter. In fact, during the match, every time Vilas hit a shot out or had trouble handling a serve or a return, he would always look up at Tiriac, and Tiriac, with that big frown of his, kept hitting the chair in front of him, as if Vilas knew exactly what Tiriac meant.

I spotted Vilas having some capuccino in that sidewalk cafe. I smiled at him and waved. He called us over to share some coffee. After a few minutes of talking about the match, I asked Vilas something I had wondered for years: "Guillermo, how is it that you're such a strong player? How do you win so often and consistently play such great tennis? What gives you that 'killer instinct' to put the ball away and to play so hard?"

What he said was a total surprise to me and, I think, to the other people at the table. Vilas said that he'd rather sniff daisies and read poetry than play tennis, and the only reason he got out there was because he just enjoyed the game and it made some money for him.

I wasn't satisfied with that answer. I asked Vilas again, "How do you play so well? How do you consistently win so many matches?"

He became serious then, and finally he said, "Kerry, you know there's really no difference between the way I play and the way a low-ranked pro plays. In fact, on any given day, any other pro could probably beat me."

But, he continued, "The reason I'm better than some of the other top players on the circuit, the reason I win so much, is because in 1975, I decided my goal was to win the French Open three years later, in 1978. It was a time when my tennis career was really blossoming, but yet I wasn't winning any of the great tournaments."

He went on, "Kerry, it's not enough just to decide you want to win a match such as the French Open. I wanted to ensure that I really would win that tournament, so I began planning. In 1977, my goal was to win the Italian Open. In 1976, my goal was to play on the Grand Prix and win tournaments in Munich and also in Rome."

Vilas said he wanted to know positively that he would win all those tournaments and that he calculated every month exactly what tournaments he had to win on a world-class circuit. Every week he knew how long he had to practice to win those satellite tournaments to ultimately be able to win the world-class tournaments. He set a game plan for himself. He would have practice sessions from 8 in the morning until 12 noon. Then he'd resume from 1 until 5 every day that he didn't have a tournament.

He said the secret of laying a plan like this was merely working backwards from the goal to the present. He knew exactly how much effort he had to put in, how much work he would have to do, to win the French Open in 1978. So he worked backwards and laid a plan for himself that couldn't fail, given his talent and given how hard he was prepared to work to achieve his objective.

Vilas said, "Kerry, most people spend more time planning a vacation than they do their lives. They spend more time deciding what they want to do on a weekend that to what they want to accomplish during any given month or year.

"But think of a very simple example. Think of building a house. You envision the house you want. You decide you want a four-bedroom place with a swimming pool, a veranda, and a good view of the mountains or lake nearby. The architect then takes your ideas—your goal—and translates them into a workable plan, which he calls a 'blueprint.' Can you imagine the builder building without a blueprint—without a game plan? Many times builders do not stay on schedule, but they at least know what they have to do next."

LAYING YOUR FRAMEWORK

By the time you finish reading *Peak Performance Selling: How to Increase Your Sales by 70% in 6 Weeks* you'll know precisely how productive you are. You'll know how many phone calls it takes for you to get an appointment, how many appointments fall through before you get to see a client, and how many times you have to see a client or a prospect to get a product sold. You'll be able to apply this to goals and activities like weight loss or child discipline.

Laying a framework or plan for yourself to achieve a goal is a fundamental element of your productivity program, but there are other important methods to use to increase your productivity.

One method is finding ways to stay on a game plan. This is the only way any of us can ever hope to achieve anything of substance. In business, when you buy a capital asset, you borrow money from a bank. The bank promptly lays a plan in which, hopefully, you can easily pay back the loan you used to buy that asset.

When using a budget, you understand exactly how much money you need to make per month and per year to survive in the business. You have a good idea of accounts receivables and payables. You know what the breakeven points are, as well as the profitability of each sale.

You probably already go into a lot of detail when planning out business goals. Why not use the same approach in your personal life for achieving business and personal objects.

I recently spoke to a realtor who took part in a peak performance selling seminar I was running. He had decided to double his activity, and thereby double the number of sales that he was making.

Well, obviously, when you're working eight hours a day, doubling your activity and then hoping to double your sales means that you're pushing yourself hard. After only two weeks on his productivity program, I met with this realtor. He told me he had become more efficient in listening to his prospects. He tried to make better use of his time, and he was making more referral contacts instead of cold calls. He also said he was attending more seminars on property financing and on marketing development.

In short, he was pushing himself, but at the same time he was finding easier ways to achieve the end result of doubling his sales. He used less activity to increase his productivity. He was becoming more efficient and effective at what he was doing.

The *law of forced efficiency* says the more you force yourself to increase your activity, the more efficient you will become and the more easily money will come to you.

If you are a manager, ask yourself these questions

What will you do differently to reach your goal?
What do you need to do to achieve that goal when you want it?

If you're a manager, specify the goal you want to achieve, and write down the amount of time you'll spend on the duties you'll do on a daily basis to achieve that objective.

If you're a manager, I also encourage you to remember the *law of imminent survival*, which states that you'll burn yourself out if you work too hard. You'll lose enthusiasm and interest in your job if you work too many hours trying to achieve an objective. I heartily encourage managers around the country to learn how to be efficiently productive enough to work eight-hour days. There is no glory in working ten to twelve hours a day. It only suggests you aren't sharp enough to delegate and manage the right way. Try to learn how to leave your work at the office and be effective enough to work a normal day.

Just knowing averages and your activity levels, however, is not enough. Knowing how much effort you need to expend to increase your activity and achieve the goal when you want it is only one part. You must also learn ways of maintaining that activity to keep your productivity level high, instead of raising your activity for one or two days and dropping back down to what you had been comfortable with.

Keeping that activity high can be accomplished through something called *habit pattern conditioning*.

In chapter 13—on habits and habit patterns—you'll be given information not only about how to condition yourself, but also about how to determine what your habit patterns are, how you can eliminate them, and how you can change virtually anything in your basic work-style to suit the way you would like to perform. You will learn ways not only of conditioning yourself, but also of understanding basic human behavior and why people do what they do.

13

What Stimulates You?
Habits and Habit Patterns:
Your Immediate and
Deferred Reward System

HOW TO MAKE CHANGES FOR MORE PRODUCTIVITY

Everything we think, do, or say is learned. We learned how to behave by receiving meaningful rewards for exhibiting particular behaviors. To make the changes we want in our behavior so we can achieve greater productivity, it is important to understand the structure of *habits* and how they can be formed and modified.

REWARDS AND PUNISHMENTS

We work for *rewards* such as money, recognition, or status. We jog because it feels good, or we enjoy it because it gives us firmer bodies and more endurance. We are polite to people because we want them to be polite to us or to like us.

Everything we do results from striving to receive some sort of reward.

We try to avoid things that serve as *punishments* or which leave us with negative feelings.

Whether it's speeding or parking tickets, we try to avoid any kind of fine associated with vehicular violations, so we abide by traffic codes. We make right turns only when we're supposed to; we park only in designated parking areas; or we drive carefully and obey state laws and rules of the road because we don't want to be fined if a policeman happens to catch us.

A traffic fine is a form of punishment. Our tendency to avoid punishment and desire rewards is the prime psychological motivation for everything we do.

Every habit we have was formed by being rewarded for an action, or being rewarded for a behavior. Punishment, on the other hand, is the most prevalent technique people use on others to change their habits. But punishment causes resentment and ill feelings. The habit or behavior may change, but only because the person wants to avoid punishment, not because the person really wants to change.

Remember: *We try to avoid punishment.*

We can try to eliminate habits or behaviors with punishment, but this usually causes resentment, distrust, and anxiety in the person being punished.

137

This is one reason why harsh, disciplinarian, punishment-oriented parents often rear misfits and social dropouts. Their children see the parents as "the establishment." They end up resenting and distrusting the authority of not only their parents, but of other authority figures in society. If you treat your children with kindness and warmth, however, they'll probably see other authority figures in society as benign.

BEHAVIOR SHAPING

Your parents rewarded you when you made your bed in the morning by saying, "Thank you," or, when you did your homework, by giving you permission to do something like go out and play baseball or football with your friends.

Your parents were getting you into the habit of making your bed or doing your homework by giving you praise or by letting you go out and play baseball, but only *after* you had accomplished the task they wanted you to.

These examples involve *behavior shaping*. Since adults are really just grown children, the same mechanisms that were used to shape our behaviors as children can be and are also used to shape our behaviors as adults. We can also use behavior shaping to get others to act the way we want them to.

After I give a seminar presentation, the attendees might line up to thank me. This response serves to reward me and reinforce whatever I've said during that program. If I told a story during my presentation that they especially liked, and they complimented me on it, the chances of my telling that story again are very high. My attendees are shaping the way I give presentations, or shaping my speaking behavior, by complimenting me and thus rewarding me with praise for the things they like.

They might also decide to punish me by telling me they don't like a part of my presentation. Their punishment serves to make me analyze that portion of the program and make changes, or perhaps decide not to tell a particular story at all.

ENVIRONMENTAL CONDITIONING

Even if we think we are totally self-controlled, we really are slowly being conditioned and manipulated by our environment. Wouldn't it be nice to be able to control yourself the same way your environment is controlling you every day?

Let me give you an example of this. Please complete the following sentences: "Try it, you'll —— —."

If you said, "like it," you've been conditioned.

Here's another one: "Ask and you shall ———."

If you thought, "receive," you've been conditioned to respond with the rest of a particular phrase after you hear a few words.

"Two and two equals ——." Even though your response to this simple equation may appear to be from memory, it's on the tip of your tongue and you've been conditioned to have an immediate response of "four."

Here's another one: "Seven-Up is the un- ——."

If you said "cola" here, you've been conditioned by television and other factors in the outside environment.

All the responses you gave to the phrases I prompted you with are examples of habit patterns. These habit patterns, in most cases have been *subliminally*, or without your conscious knowledge, conditioned in you like an instant reflex or knee jerk.

Your immediate feeling now is probably that you're being controlled by your environment, controlled by the television set, controlled by your friends, controlled by all the things around you—and you're right. Yet, without habit patterns, life itself would be virtually impossible.

THE IMPORTANCE OF HABIT PATTERNS

Habit patterns help you make routine decisions. When you get home after a hard day's work, you don't stand in your doorway trying to decide what you should do first. Your habits work to help you walk in, take your jacket off, sit down, and read the newspaper without having to think about it.

Habit patterns are important because they help to keep us productive. Without habit patterns, we would be confused much of the time. Just consider the amount of time lost if we had to stop and decide what to do first, second, and so on in the morning routine—whether to go to the bathroom first or put on our slippers. Think about your own morning habits. Consider how awkward and confusing it would be to do them out of the sequence you have established over the years.

Our habits increase our productivity when we are communicating or interacting with someone. When someone talks to you, you listen. And, when they're done you say, "I understand," or "I have a question."

You respond, thereby rewarding them by confirming that you were listening. You don't both talk at the same time. You have been conditioned to either listen or speak.

In many cases, you've also been conditioned by the outside environment to smile when you first meet someone. Another familiar example of a conditioned habit is to respond with "Fine, thank you," when someone asks, "How are you?"

These habits actually aid us and increase our productivity by keeping communication channels open and also enabling us to have good social skills.

If we didn't have habits, life itself would be extremely dangerous. If we didn't have a conditioned habit pattern when driving a car on a freeway, for example, we might change lanes at the drop of a hat, or turn off the freeway from the left lane when the turnoff is on the right side of the road.

We all know someone with very bad driving habits. He or she may go ninety or even a hundred miles an hour, making it very dangerous for other people on the road, especially those who go 30 or 40 miles per hour. When driving, a habit pattern is necessary and mandatory.

Habit patterns also give our lives social order. We have a good idea of how other people are going to react in situations. In most cases, if we're nice to people, they in turn are nice back. In most cases, we can predict with a fair amount of accuracy that people won't fly off the handle at the drop of a hat and throw things or shoot people. Although there is some evidence that these habit patterns do break down with psychotic or schizophrenic individuals, by and large if we smile at somebody, they'll smile back. If we frown at somebody, they'll frown back.

Habits help us function smoothly in our lives. They help us lead productive, predictable lives. Habits tend to prevent confusion.

THE ROOTS OF HABIT PATTERNS

Habits are extremely tough to break, mainly because they're tough to form. The whole process of change, or of modifying habits, is one of the most difficult things we can ever do. The process of change causes stress and thereby causes discomfort, either in the form of anxiety or depression.

One of the reasons most of us don't stick to our New Year's resolutions is basically because of the anxiety change brings us when we start to modify our habits.

When I played professional tennis, for example, I had a very smooth, very accurate backhand, but it wasn't always that way. When I was learning how to play tennis at the age of five, I had an enormous problem learning both the forehand and backhand, and at the ages of eight and nine, I remember hitting with my backhand, sometimes as much as two to three hours a day. At a young age, that's a very high amount of activity.

But after about two to three months of hitting my backhand and practicing hard, I found something called *muscle memory* came into play. I didn't have to concentrate on getting my racket low, leading with my shoulder, moving into the ball—all those things came very naturally without my having to even so much as think about them.

In time, just like muscle memory, habits tend to become entrenched. Be aware also that sometimes our entrenched habit patterns can hurt us or sabotage our efforts in working toward an objective.

How are habit patterns formed? To answer this, you'll need to know a little about human behavior.

HUMAN BEHAVIOR RESULTS FROM REWARDS AND PUNISHMENTS

As we said earlier, human behavior results from rewards given to us or punishments inflicted on us. All of us tend to seek rewards for activities we do, and all of us tend to flee from punishment.

If you had a girlfriend or boyfriend who was very appreciative of you, very complimentary and affectionate, you would want to be around that person often. You may buy her or him things to indicate you like her or him. You may be as nice as you can be to that special person.

If this person told you what a jerk you were whenever you made a mistake, or was constantly deprecating you, you would probably try to replace the person within a very short period of time. When the person was complimentary, or rewarded you, she or he caused you to feel more accepted and closer in the relationship because you seek rewards just as you seek to avoid punishment or people who are inflicting punishment on you.

Rewards and punishments affect almost every aspect of our lives. If we go to a grocery store, and it is constantly crowded, we'll probably go to another. We find the crowdedness of the grocery store punishing or aversive. We tend to avoid such situations.

But if you went to a gas station and, even though prices might be a little higher than at other stations, if the attendant was very thorough in doing your windshield, checked your tires, filled your tank with a smile on his face, and was very congenial and easy to get along with, that is a very rewarding experience and you would probably go back week after week.

Every habit we currently have was formed by being rewarded for an action. For example, if you brought donuts to your secretary one morning, and she not only told you how much she liked you bringing them, but she also tended to work harder and more efficiently, you would probably bring donuts every morning from then on, thereby creating a habit of going to the local donut store to bring those donuts to work. In time, you would instill new work habits in your secretary because you were rewarding her.

PARENTAL REWARDS AND PEER REINFORCEMENT

When you were a child, your habits were established by your parents with *parental rewards* and your peers with *peer reinforcement*.

Think back for a moment. If your peer group used words like "groovy," didn't you also use such words because you wanted to be accepted by your group? They in turn would reward you by letting you be a part of their group.

As children, our habits were constantly established or changed by peer reinforcement. We all wore the same type of T-shirts. All of our friends wore Levis, so we wore Levis too. Or we wore the same brand of tennis shoes.

The reward, or reinforcement, was basically acceptance from our peer group. We wanted them to like us. They showed they did like us as a reward for dressing, acting, or speaking like a part of the group.

Parents also reinforced our behaviors or rewarded habits when we were very young by giving us an allowance or a reward for mowing the lawn or cleaning our room. Because perhaps you received 50 cents for mowing the lawn once a week, it increased the likelihood that you would also mow the lawn next week and the week after that, or do the dishes one night, or even rake the leaves. Soon a habit pattern would be established. Even if you didn't receive the allowance as often, you would still mow the lawn or rake the leaves in anticipation of the reward.

Many parents use rewards with their children very appropriately. One parent I know occasionally buys her son a favorite toy just because he sweeps the driveway daily. This random reward works well because the mother tells the child why he is getting the toy. Since he never knows when to expect it, he tends to sweep the driveway daily, anticipating he might be rewarded with a toy.

Many habits our parents instill in us as children are the basic habits we need to use to deal effectively with life's minor concerns, such as how to tie a shoe, button a shirt or blouse, or brush our teeth.

INTERMITTENT, IMMEDIATE, AND DEFERRED REWARDS

In real-life applications, *intermittent rewards* are prevalent in places like casinos. Slot machines are one of the most addictive vices around. One reason for this is that when we use a slot machine, we're rewarded when three oranges or three lemons come up on the slot machine window. The machine gives us ten times the amount of money we put in the machine.

The slot machine does not reward us every time we put another quarter in, but perhaps every tenth, twentieth, or even one-hundredth time. This intermittent reward is enough to keep us playing that slot machine. You always feel the next time will be your big win.

Receiving what is called an intermittent reward keeps us gambling. In fact, in many cases it causes a habit to be established. If you see a slot machine and think you will try it "just once," chances are you will keep feeding coins in the slot.

We do things to get *immediate rewards*, like getting a point every time we win in a tennis game. We also work for *deferred rewards*, such as the revenue yielded by a long-term investment after a year or two. Both types of rewards can be used to establish, modify, or break habits. The more immediately we give ourselves or someone gives us a reward for an activity, the greater the chance the activity will become a habit. That's because we basically tend to do activities which give us the most immediate rewards.

For example, if you bought your spouse roses and as soon as you presented them you received a kiss, you would probably do it again. But if you presented the roses and it took a week or two before you were told how nice they were, you probably wouldn't buy roses anymore or at least not very frequently.

A lot of us avoid doing things which give us deferred rewards, like starting a new business. Businesses usually have an initial start-up period of about two years. One of the reasons why most individuals don't make it in business is because they don't have the patience to wait for rewards such as high income, freedom, and less work, because it takes so long to get these things. They have made the mistake of only setting the goal— establishing a business—without planning the steps to get there, the work they must do to get the goal, and the appropriate rewards they might receive along the way.

Salespeople usually intensely dislike prospecting or digging up new business on the telephone. If the salesperson can receive an immediate reward, however, such as eating a piece of his or her favorite candy or fruit or some other treat that is enjoyed after each phone call is made, those calls become less disliked and more enjoyable. They also become much closer to a habit, because making the phone call is rewarded by receiving a piece of candy or fruit.

A salesperson I worked with a short time ago at a major stock brokerage company intensely disliked prospecting. In fact, he disliked it to the point that, even though his business was sinking so badly that he probably wouldn't survive in the investment industry, he still wouldn't make either referral calls or cold calls.

I asked him what he liked to eat. He told me he enjoyed bananas. So I got the idea of linking the reward of one small piece of banana to every phone call made.

He told me that about a month later, after using the banana as a reward, his cold calls and referral calls increased 150 percent. Every time he made a phone call, he'd give himself a small piece of banana, so he was really working for the bite of fruit. Nonetheless, he still was able to associate a pleasurable experience, such as eating the fruit, with a nonpleasurable experience like the phone call. Making the phone calls began to be much more enjoyable.

While most of us don't enjoy directly prospecting or making phone calls because the people we call often aren't nice or very polite to us, if we give ourselves a reward for doing this undesirable activity, we can usually increase the amount of phone calls we make.

Rewards can be applied in virtually any situation where we want to change habits or modify behavior. My son has a problem picking up his toys. He leaves toys in the living room and scattered about his bedroom. Since asking him to pick up his toys doesn't work, and yelling at him has an equally useless effect, we started him on a program in which he receives 25 cents as a reward every day that he picks up all his toys without being asked.

This reward of 25 cents is a tremendously effective technique which totally solidifies as well as establishes his habit of picking up his toys. The only reason this really works, however, is because he places money at a very high value, mainly because he can buy what he wants with the money and not have to ask us for toys. He has the freedom to purchase what he wants.

If you want to cause a behavior to become a habit, reward yourself for the behavior after you do it.

PROMOTING BEHAVIORS INTO HABITS

If we can do or promote a certain behavior, such as making prospecting calls consistently for three to four weeks—21 to 31 days—it will become a habit. But new behaviors must be done on a regular basis.

Habits work against us, too. Most of us don't realize that if we go to work late—perhaps five or ten minutes every day for one month straight—a habit will form. It will set in much like molding putty sets and dries. It's very difficult to change the shape of the putty once it does dry, just as it's difficult to change a habit once it's established. Bad habits are much easier to start or initiate than they are to break.

In fact, some very prestigious psychological researchers say that habits are never really broken--that we just put new habits in their place.

Doing anything repeatedly for 21 to 30 days is really all it takes to put a new habit in place. For example, I enjoy reading very much. It's also crucial to my business. But I usually find it very difficult to take the time to read. To encourage myself to read, I reward myself, usually in the evening, with small sips of root beer, which I enjoy very much. This root beer acts as a reinforcer or a reward. I give myself this root beer for every page I turn.

I used the reward of getting the sip of root beer for every page turned for approximately 21 days. After the 21-day period, even though I didn't drink the root beer anymore with reading, I developed a habit of reading nightly. The habit solidified within that three-week period, and I continued to read almost every night from then on, even without the root beer. If I wasn't able to read, I felt that I had missed something that day, like you would feel if you hadn't brushed your teeth before going to bed at night.

The only way to change or modify our habit patterns is to use a reward-based conditioning technique, such as the one I've been describing.

ELIMINATING HABITS WITH PUNISHMENT

A habit is eliminated if you receive punishment for it. If you received an electric shock when you put your key in the front door of your home, it wouldn't be long before you'd use the back door. Or if the roses you brought home to your spouse went unacknowledged or were ill-received, it wouldn't be long before you stopped bringing roses, and probably stopped bringing presents in general.

It's very difficult for a behavior to become a habit or stay a habit, if you receive no enjoyment when you do it or if you are laughed at or embarrassed or reprimanded when you take part in it. Punishment does not help form habits, but it helps break them.

For example, think of speeding down the highway in your car. This is extremely dangerous and not very fuel-efficient. But many people enjoy driving very fast. In time, this behavior of speeding becomes a habit. In fact, you soon would probably feel that driving slowly is boring and not at all enjoyable. You find the habit of speeding to be enjoyable, exciting, and just a lot of fun.

Fortunately, the habit of speeding is dealt with very effectively by Highway Patrol officers. They punish you by using techniques like giving you traffic tickets, and being very demeaning and condescending when they talk to you. Eventually, when you go see a traffic court judge, you're punished with a fine.

If you find it particularly fun to speed and ignore the fine—the punishment you get—then, if you are caught again by a Highway Patrol officer, you are what is called a "repeat offender" (what authorities really mean by this is that you are not responding well to punishment), and they deal with you by imposing more strict fines: more money, perhaps even jail. They give you tougher and tougher punishments, hoping that your habit of speeding will be eliminated.

Punishment, or not getting a reward for a habit, is very useful in eliminating habits or behavior patterns, but

punishment is not at all useful in forming habits.

For example, if your spouse has a habit of leaving the car lights on when returning from having taken out the family car, complaining will probably stop your spouse from the habit of leaving the lights on. But he or she will also probably intensely dislike you for the chiding; it'll cause marital strife; and your spouse may even think of ways to get back at you for your scolding or condescending behavior.

If, on the other hand, you give your spouse a reward for having remembered to turn the lights off, perhaps a hug or kiss or maybe doing some extra household chores, not only would you shape in your spouse a habit of turning the car lights off but your spouse would also probably enjoy being with you much more, and would probably show it through happiness or gratitude.

The point is,

while punishment does work to eliminate certain behaviors or habits, giving a reward usually works twice as fast to form a new habit.

For the most part, habits are not really eliminated, but rather replaced with new ones.

The same thing is true with children. If your child runs outside without putting on a jacket on a cold day, screaming at the child will probably work. It will probably keep the child from going without a jacket. But you'll probably have to scream each time. By giving your child an enjoyable reward, such as praise, affection, or candy for putting on a jacket will usually work extremely well, plus your child will grow up to be much happier and well-adjusted, and feel confident, with higher self-esteem. The child will also be much more loving, affectionate, and admiring of you as the parent.

Punishment may have its place, but it's used much too often in our society to try to eliminate habits or change people's behaviors. To change behaviors and create habits, rewards work much more efficiently and effectively than punishment could ever hope to. The basic end result of punishment is really to enable the punisher to vent his or her anger or frustration.

Punishment never has formed and never will form a habit pattern. A husband might say to his wife, "Why don't you have dinner on the table when I come home? I don't know why I ever married you." The husband should know that criticism only causes emotions of distress, anger, and rejection in his wife, and does not serve to change her behavior.

Parents often tend to make the great mistake of using punishment to try to reinforce and establish behaviors. "Tommy, you're so stupid you'll never learn to tie your own shoes."

You probably can sense why anxiety, rejection, and discouragment set in, making it very likely that Tommy will not only not learn to tie his shoes appropriately, but he will also feel dislike and anxiety toward his parents.

Consider two things

1. Are you spending too much time punishing others—your family and friends—for inappropriate behavior instead of rewarding them for appropriate behavior?
2. Are you punishing or rewarding yourself?

Punishing yourself can be as devastating as having someone else punish you. In 1978, when I was on the Grand Prix Tennis Tour, I frequently, in the middle of a tennis match, would berate myself because of bad shots I was hitting. I was punishing myself because I didn't like the way I was playing.

But when I was in Monte Carlo in Europe, I was able to play the number three rated tennis player from Argentina. We were playing on a clay court surface, which I wasn't used to. Being from California, I was used to a fast serve and volley on a hard court surface. Every time I missed a ball, I'd say to myself, "You idiot! Can't you do anything right?"

And every time I'd miss, I'd berate myself more and more and get more angry and more upset.

But, as you might have guessed, the more angry I became at myself, the more upset I became, and the worse I did. There tends to be a snowball effect, until you finally do exactly what you predicted you would—poorly. It becomes a self-fulfilling prophecy.

"You idiot! I knew you couldn't hit that ball."

I was losing. But then I decided to change tactics. In the middle of the second set of a three-set match, I stopped punishing myself for my bad shots. I began by giving myself a sip of water every time I hit a winner. I'd go to the sidelines very briefly and take a sip of water, and then go right back onto the court.

While this was a bit irregular because it slowed down the tennis match, I found that by giving myself rewards or reinforcements, my confidence was built up. I also played better because I was giving myself a reward after every point. I started congratulating myself. I started giving myself encouragment for the good shots that I made, while just ignoring the bad ones.

INCREASING PERFORMANCE WITH REWARD

You can increase your performance and productivity if you do the very simple thing of rewarding rather than punishing yourself, building confidence in yourself instead of trying to convince yourself how bad or worthless you are at doing basic things or trying to achieve what you want in your life. The foundation of your whole sales performance program really rests on the issues of building self-esteem and self-confidence.

It's important to understand basic human behavior, habits, and habit patterns before you can ever attempt to make any changes in yourself. By understanding how you influence and control others with rewards and punishments and how they control you, the next chapters—on discriminative stimuli, the psychology of change, and how you can modify your own behavior to increase your productivity—will be much more meaningful. You'll have clearer insight into potential sales performance barriers and know how you can remove them.

By the time you finish reading *Peak Performance Selling: How to Increase Your Sales by 70% in 6 Weeks*, you'll have the information to create a reward-based conditioning technique that can help you vastly increase the amount of money you are now making, the amount of weight you want to lose, and the cooperation you can get from children, peers, or subordinates. You'll virtually be able to condition a change in any habit or behavior you choose.

Most important, if you follow your tailor-made performance program, your sales can increase dramatically within 6 to 8 weeks.

14

How Good Are You? Analyzing and Comparing Current Production to Future Needs

Are there times when you feel depressed for no apparent reason? Or do you feel anxious or nervous in certain situations, like meeting with lawyers, but feel fine meeting with others, like accountants? Or do you feel strange or even upset or anxious just walking into your office or sitting at your desk?

On the other hand, do you get a comfortable, warm feeling as soon as you get home after a long day? Does something specific happen that gives you this feeling as soon as you take a step into the doorway of your house? Does your spouse greet you with a smile and a kiss? Or do your kids immediately give you a hug and tell you how much they love you? Probably not.

Why do our emotions change drastically just because we're in a different place or in a meeting with different people? Even though people have not yet spoken to us, why do we tend to feel good or very suspicious and hostile toward them, perhaps just because of the way they are dressed?

DISCRIMINATIVE STIMULUS

In my work, I've heard various businesspeople say, "I felt uncomfortable as soon as I walked into his office. I don't know what it was, but I felt very ill at ease," or "It was one of the warmest places I've ever been. I couldn't spot anything different about his office than anybody else's, but it was just a place I wanted to get back to."

The "difference" lies in the psychological explanation called a *discriminative stimulus*, or *environmental conditioning*, which we discussed briefly in chapter 13. The underlying idea of discriminative stimuli is that our feelings of comfort or discomfort with people like lawyers, or in places like highways or our offices, are really dependent on our experience.

If we had only worked with lawyers who had been demeaning, condescending, or continually made us feel subhuman, then we would quickly become conditioned to feel uncomfortable as soon as we stepped into a lawyer's office. If we had a difficult problem at one time with a particular lawyer, for example—perhaps he or she made us feel very stupid—we probably came away from that meeting feeling like we didn't want to see this lawyer—or any lawyer—again.

In fact, if we had gone into another lawyer's office the following week, our feelings of discomfort would probably still have been there. Our feelings would start becoming generalized. We would start to feel uncomfortable being in any lawyer's office. Even though another lawyer had said nothing, or perhaps had only said, "Hello, how are you?" our suspicion and apprehension would be easily aroused because of our last experience with a lawyer.

The opposite may be true of our homes. If we feel sudden joy or comfort as soon as we walk into our house, it's probably because our spouses makes us feel very wonderful, like a special person, even though they may not even be around when we open the door. But we remember the good feelings of being in the house, which is a strong contrast to the anxiety we experience from a hard day at work.

If our spouse doesn't give us joy, and we still feel good being home, our reaction is a little bit more complex. Home is probably just the lesser of two evils—the greater evil being our work and daily rigor. Even though home may not an especially nice place to be, we still feel better being there than we do taking the knocks at the office all day long.

OVERCOMING IRRATIONAL FEARS

Understanding how discriminative stimuli and environmental conditioning work can give us insight into why many times we feel distressed or anxious about making calls or going to somebody's office. We can begin to understand that we really are just conditioned to feel distressed by our experience.

Simple stress management techniques can help us cope with stress and anxiety. These techniques can help us get rid of our *irrational fears* which may have resulted from environmental conditioning.

Let's say, for example, that yesterday, Monday, you may have made ten phone calls, but with each phone call you made you experienced severe rejection. Today is Tuesday, and if you still can't get up enough enthusiasm or motivation to make more phone calls, you have probably been environmentally conditioned by Monday's rejection (or some earlier day's rejection) to anticipate feeling rejected whenever you're around the phone, maybe even whenever you approach your desk.

A good solution in this case might be to do something as simple as, after making a phone call to a prospect, immediately calling your spouse or a good friend as a reward to decrease anxiety. If calling your spouse or friend produces comfort, it will help decrease anxiety, and should drive down your chances of feeling rejected.

If meeting in a lawyer's or an accountant's office makes you anxious, doing something as simple as getting a milkshake on your way home from those meetings, or stopping off at a friend's office could help relieve the stress or anxiety you felt being in that office.

We all feel distress being in certain places or around certain things that remind us of problems or of situations that gave us anxiety. When we experience this distress again, we need to rid ourselves of it so we don't generalize and associate it with similar places or things. We may be feeling uncomfortable with a particular lawyer who gave us stress; we shouldn't feel uncomfortable with every member of the legal profession.

USING REWARDS: "DE-STRESSING" TECHNIQUES

Knowing about environmental conditioning can help us overcome a lot of fears and anxieties we may experience in our business lives right now.

One salesperson I worked with experienced call reluctance. He had an intense fear of calling customers. (See chapter 9 for more on overcoming call reluctance.) His fear was basically because he had become environmentally conditioned due to past bad experiences on the telephone. He felt anxious and somewhat distressed as soon as he even looked at the telephone.

But by giving himself rewards for phone calls, as well as, between business calls, calling friends or acquaintances whom he got along with well, he was able to dissipate his fear and increase his phone call activity. He was basically preventing anxiety. He now can make ten referral calls a day. He is qualifying properly, so every phone call can be important to him if he chooses to follow up on it. In most cases he does.

That instrument of terror, the telephone—the tool that had given him such anxiety in the past—is now something he can cope with very easily. As a result of the "de-stressing" technique of talking to a friend in between prospect calls, or even talking to another individual in the office in between prospect calls, he was able to totally dispel his fear of the telephone and of the rejection he was getting.

I worked on an interesting case with a husband who was having great difficulty developing any enthusiasm being around his wife. The individual, a manager in a very prestigious firm, had been married for two or three years. Every time he went home, he felt like going to sleep. He felt almost no ambition or motivation to do anything with his wife, or even to talk to her.

This was not always the case. In fact, he confided to me that during the first year of marriage all he always wanted to do was take his wife to dinner, talk to her about his business or what had happened during the day, and spend virtually his whole evening communicating about plans or concerns they had for the future.

The husband told me that after this first year he and his wife had had a series of terrible confrontations in which she had screamed and thrown things at him. He had reacted similarly to her. After about six months, the marital conflicts died out, but he said he was left with a true feeling of lethargy, or lack of motivation, whenever he was around her.

He had been conditioned by their frequent arguments and fights to avoid his wife. When he was around her, he would be quiet. And basically, he would not go out of his way to try to entertain her for fear that the arguments would once again erupt.

Even though he said he wanted to pay more attention to her, and felt much better toward her than he had during that six-month conflict period, he had great difficulty finding any joy being around her at all.

This is a classic case of environmental conditioning. For a period of time, he had received so much punishment and stress from one person that it became difficult for him to feel positive or good toward that person later on, even though he felt he wanted to be positive, friendly, or even loving toward that person.

I once counseled a woman who had difficulty being around tall men with dark hair and dark moustaches. She told me that she had had an extremely bad relationship with a man who was tall and had dark hair and a moustache. The relationship had ended when the boyfriend began physically abusing her. She had been in the hospital for two or three days because of abrasions on the face and bruises and lacerations on her body.

From then on, even in business, she was extremely suspicious of tall, dark-haired men with moustaches, to the point where she didn't like to be in the room or an office alone with a man with those characteristics, nor did she feel comfortable about even working with such an individual. Her environmental conditioning caused her to generalize her discomfort to a whole group of men.

We are environmentally conditioned in our offices by the telephone or by experiences with clients, and with other professionals, such as lawyers and accountants. At home we are environmentally conditioned by our families.

Very often people who are environmentally conditioned will generalize things. Perhaps because we had a bad experience with the president of a company we will leave that company, saying to ourselves, "I'll never talk to a president again."

This type of generalizing is something we all do or we all feel. We generalize because we fear the same problem we had in the past will occur again under similar present circumstances.

We can overcome an environmentally conditioned response by using some simple relaxation or stress-coping techniques, such as rewarding ourselves with reinforcers when we begin to overcome the generalized fears, or by using the progressive relaxation technique as described in chapter 8.

Progressive relaxation can help us relieve the tension we experience from anxiety-producing situations. Remember: progressive relaxation involves the simple exercise of imagining yourself in someplace that gives you solitude, like a wooded forest. Imagine yourself going into a peaceful, wooded forest. Spend approximately five minutes imagining yourself walking into the forest, about twenty minutes in the forest, and five minutes walking out. Do this by yourself in a quiet room in a very comfortable chair. Loosen your tie or unbutton your top blouse button and relax as much as you can.

You can then use the progressive relaxation technique during the day whenever you find yourself anxious or suffering from an environmentally conditioned response. Set aside ninety seconds to two minutes. Have your secretary hold your calls. Take about three deep breaths and exhale slowly. Visualize yourself back in the forest for just about one minute, take three more breaths and go back to work. You'll be amazed at how well this works to get rid of anxieties and helps to increase your productivity.

15

Applying Rewards to the Game Plan: Changing Target Production Behavior Patterns

In chapter 13, we talked about how our habits and habit patterns are developed as a result of being rewarded for particular behavior patterns. Here, we will show how rewards and reinforcers can be used to help us reach target behavior patterns on the road to great sales performance.

It is a fact that we do everything to achieve a reward or to avoid a punishment. Many psychologists have based their life's work on this premise. To a great extent, we strive extremely hard to receive those things which are pleasurable, gratifying, or reinforcing. We also spend a good deal of time avoiding those things that bring us punishment.

The law of effect holds that all organisms, including human beings, are governed by the consequences of their own behavior. If the consequences are rewarding we tend to engage in those behaviors which yield rewards again and again. If those consequences are unrewarding, we tend to cease from engaging in that behavior in the future.

REWARDS AND REINFORCERS

Behavioral psychologists claim there are two types of rewards that affect our behavior

1. *Simple rewards* such as eating, sleeping, and sex.
2. *Complex rewards* such as a child's toys, praise, attention, compliments, as well as cars and money.

Complex rewards are very powerful. But they may be extremely difficult to recognize since they vary in effectiveness from person to person. One salesperson may make lots of phone calls because he enjoys phone calls and thinks they are rewarding. Another may make them because he wants to avoid the punishment of his manager threatening termination. It could also be that the salesperson realizes that she'll make a bigger sale, her reward, if she makes those phone calls now.

The consequence of a behavior is termed its reward. Rewards increase the likelihood that a certain behavior will be repeated. They can yield positive or remove negative behavior.

There are some rewards that are reinforcing for practically everyone, like food, water, air, or other substances vital to our survival. But the reason some individuals desire a particular reward is sometimes a mystery.

My eleven-year-old son, Neil, for example, loves a kind of music which would be considered torture by many civilizations. His pre-teenage favorites include music with a hard driving beat and scratchy, irritating high-pitched guitar chords. Whenever we get into the car, he will take at least three to four minutes to set the radio to his favorite station, usually erasing from memory my preset radio station. At the same time, he has difficulty understanding why I want to listen to soft jazz as well as why I enjoy non-acid rock music.

If Neil isn't allowed to listen to his music in the car he thinks of it as punishment. He will typically gripe and grouse over how unfair I am to him and tell me what a lousy parent I am. He is not given his music as a reward so he feels punished.

For something to qualify as a reward or *reinforcer* depends on a number of things

How important is that reward?

How do we feel at the time we receive it?

Who is giving us the reward?

For example, if as a salesperson you get a reward of $10 every time you make a particular type of phone call, the chances of you making another phone call are greatly enhanced. *That* reward has a high degree of importance and will directly relate to how much you want that $10 bill.

On the other hand, if you receive a grape or candy bar after every phone call, you will soon become satiated with those rewards. It will become less reinforcing. It won't be long before you stop making the phone calls because of your lack of motivation.

The reward obviously needs to be important. It also needs to be frequent. Once you've received a reward for one activity, however, it will directly affect the type of reward you desire for other activities as well.

I travel around the country a lot. Many weeks I travel more than 8,000 miles, which is nothing compared to how far my baggage travels. While I'm away, my wife, Sandy, dispenses her own system of rewards and punishments to our children. Her idea of punishment is to yell and threaten when she is upset at their behavior. Her idea of reward is to give the children practically anything they want.

When Sandy asks Neil, our son, to wash the car, for instance, she usually gives him $5 since that is what she would pay if she took the car to the local car wash. For an 11-year-old, $5 in one hour is more money than most of his friends make in one week.

Rewards and Reinforcers

My payment is not as high as Sandy's. When I ask Neil to mow the lawn, for example, I'll offer $2 or $2.50. Neil counters, "Why should I mow the lawn for a couple of bucks when I can wait a week and wash Mom's car again?" Often I have to threaten him with punishment to get him to accept the reward.

I recently offered to reward Neil with $3 for every book he read. He doesn't like to read and needs to enhance his reading ability. Because Mom's reward payment schedule is higher for jobs Neil does around the house, $3 doesn't seem like a lot. Because of the frequency of getting money as a reward, the importance of small bills to Neil is not that great.

This phenomenon also frequently occurs in business. When a salesperson is used to making high commissions, but feels stifled in the job, this person has an extremely difficult time after moving to a new position. This occurs largely because most sales jobs start out on a base salary or a draw. To learn the product and the marketplace as well as the prospects, the salesperson has a difficult time at first making as much money as before. Since the frequency at which he received money from his previous job was very high, he does not see the new job as rewarding enough to make the initial sacrifice.

Rewards have an extremely high amount of control over our own basic behavior. When I speak in front of a group and they all nod their heads and smile or overtly laugh when I use some humor, the chances are increased that I will again use the same humorous line or joke at a future program. The audience, in essence, has control over what I say to them.

In many cases, an audience can make or break a good program. A responsive audience rewards a speaker, helping him or her feel more at ease. A defensive audience produces a bad or poor program by not showing emotion, causing a speaker to feel more inhibited or ill at ease and producing a less than excellent presentation.

Similarly, parents often let their children manipulate them and produce inappropriate behaviors. A small child may be crying in his bed. The parents want the child to sleep, but instead pick the child up to keep him or her from crying. The child then stops crying and consciously or unconsciously realizes that this is the way to let the parent know that he or she doesn't want to take a nap. The parents in this case have reinforced the child's behavior of crying when he or she is ill at ease or in bed.

My daughter Stacey has manipulated my wife, Sandy, in much the same way. To keep Stacey from crying when she was younger, Sandy would lie down with her in her bed until Stacey fell asleep. Then Sandy would walk out of the bedroom and go back to what she was doing previously. Now at three years old, Stacey is fully able to sleep without Sandy being with her. Unfortunately, Sandy has produced a behavior pattern in Stacey whereby Stacey can't fall asleep unless Sandy sleeps with her for at least an hour beforehand.

For the same reason, it is no small wonder why salespeople dislike paperwork so much. There are rewards for making sales, but there are no rewards for filling out the form sheets and reports needed by management to keep track of salespeoples' productivity.

An agency I consulted with recently had problems getting salespeople to get their reports in on time. My recommendation was to reward the salespeople for getting reports in on time. The company would have a beer party every Friday after work. Only those agents who filled reports out would be able to attend. Reports were not only turned in on time but were filled out much more efficiently.

One of the most interesting facets of behavioral psychology is the strange phenomenon that when rewards are given infrequently they can have a *more* powerful effect on behavior than if given out every time the desired behavior occurs. This phenomenon involves a concept called *variable ratio reinforcement*.

Variable ratio reinforcement occurs in almost every walk of life. In my own office, my secretary Marilyn realizes that if she does a good job she will get praised. Unfortunately, I am fairly inconsistent in my praise. But it has turned out to the best advantage of the business. When she's done a good job and I notice it, I will praise her which increases the likelihood that she will do a good job on similar projects again.

The interesting point is that she never knows *when* she'll get praised, only that the praise is random and based on doing a good job.

We talked about two types of rewards in chapter 13, *immediate rewards* and *deferred rewards*. The idea behind immediate rewards is that the quicker you are given a reward, the greater the chance it has to affect your behavior. For example, if I do work for a company and it results in immediate praise within minutes of completing the project, the chances I'll work on a similar project again are very high. If the praise or money for that work takes months or even years to get, I will likely refuse to work on similar projects in the future.

The California Lottery Commission is very aware of this phenomenon. They used to have something called the "daily number," whose players had to wait until the evening news to learn if their number was selected. This is a deferred reward. When sales of lottery tickets sank, the lottery commission implemented a much quicker immediate reward. They began selling "scratch-off lottery tickets," whose players bought lottery tickets, scratched a substance off the tickets, and learned if they had won. The proprietor of the store where any winning ticket was purchased awarded $5, $10, $25, or even $100 on the spot. The California commission found sales increased dramatically because of a reward's immediacy.

Deferred rewards *can* be very effective, but they must be of very great importance or value to the recipient.

When I first started my business, for example, I had to make an enormous number of sales phone calls. I would give myself immediate rewards such as a sip of coffee or some grapes or strawberries after every phone call.

But I also gave myself a deferred reward to keep myself on track. If, for example, I made enough phone calls during the day, I would reward myself in the evening with a game of tennis, one of my favorite pastimes. While it was not a reward as valued as a new house or car, I would still withhold tennis time from myself and position it as a reinforcer, thus increasing the likelihood that I would make my scheduled number of phone calls during the day.

I fully realized that if I didn't make the phone calls, my business would never take off. But by myself I didn't have the discipline to make those calls. The immediate and deferred rewards worked extremely well not only in increasing phone call behavior but also in substantially increasing my business success.

A problem with deferred rewards is that sometimes they are too far removed for the recipient to associate them with the appropriate behavior. For example, many companies offer sales incentive trips in an effort to get people to produce. In January, they may announce an incentive of a free trip to Spain, Hong Kong, or Mexico to take place the following December if the salespeople reach a certain production level.

Management assumes that the salespeople would produce more during the intervening 12 months, because they would plan to go on the trip. What often happens, however, is that the salespeople don't even think about the incentive trip until October, when it may be too late to produce enough business.

Rarely will a salesperson qualify during the months of January to March for a trip that takes place the following December. The trip is a reward that is too deferred to have any effect on behavior. Sales incentive campaigns or contests lasting one to three months are more effective.

In laboratory studies, we saw decreased deferred reward behavior when we put a rat into a cage and tested how often it would press a lever to receive a food pellet. If a rat was scheduled to receive a pellet for every nine presses, an interesting thing would happen. It would lackadaisically press the lever four to six times, press the lever very quickly the last three times, then get the food pellet. This occurred in almost every case when the rat knew how many times it would have to push the lever.

People behave much the same way. They often procrastinate in sales activity until the last minute. Then, to produce quotas, they work their rear ends off to get a deferred reward.

SUPERSTITIONS

An interesting observation that psychological researchers have made in rat behavior is that when there was a long delay after the rat pressed the lever before it got its food rewards, or when the reward or reinforcement schedule was complex, the rats would tend to engage in ritualistic behavior patterns.

For example, in the laboratory, the rat would do a flip or walk around in a circle. The rat would work this into what is known as a *schedule of reinforcement*.

Professionals in much the same way develop ritualistic behaviors or superstitions. We all have seen baseball players who approach the batter's box by digging their spikes into the turf in a particular way, then spinning the bat precisely the same number of times before setting for the pitch.

When I was on the professional tennis tour, I was told that Jimmy Connors would wear special color socks whenever he played John McEnroe. Ivan Lendl would wear only a specific style shirt when he played Boris Becker. This occured obviously because he had won against Becker when he was wearing that type of shirt so he would wear it every time he played him in the future. In other words, he thought the shirt may contribute to his winning and so wore it as part of a ritualistic behavior pattern.

When I played professional tennis, I would tie my shoes a certain way because I knew that I had won matches before with that behavior pattern. Years ago, when I played in a major tournament in La Jolla, California, I had a major win against a vastly superior player. There was no logical explanation for my 6-3, 6-2 victory, other than the opponent just had a bad day. But afterwards I unconsciously evaluated everything I wore, every step I took, and the type of serves I took, trying to pinpoint that exact behavior so I could replicate it in the future. For at least a year afterwards, I made sure that my racquet string tension was exactly 58 because that was the string tension that helped me defeat that player, along with bouncing the ball exactly two times before first serve and one time before a second serve.

I still have the ball-bouncing ritual in my tennis behavior. It is extremely difficult to get rid of ritualistic behavior. I recently tried to bounce the ball one time for a first serve and was so preoccupied with the discomfort that I ended up double faulting.

RELATIONSHIPS

The same *law of effect* governs our relationships. It is interesting to note that the amount of positive reinforcement or punishment you receive in a relationship with your spouse or friend to a large extent determines the likelihood of staying together. When the costs of a relationship or marriage outweigh the benefits, there is a greater chance of a breakup.

I recently asked a friend of mine why he broke up with his wife. At first he told me they just didn't get along together, that they both had changed. But in delving deeper, he told me that the reasons for staying together just didn't seem that important. The punishment he experienced far outweighed the rewards and reinforcers that could have caused them to stay together.

One goal of relationships is to increase the amount of positive reinforcement we receive from and give to our mate. To outweigh the punishment or cost of a relationship, we need to keep increasing the number of rewards or benefits we give to and receive from that relationship.

Sometimes people stay in bad relationships because of good memories. The memories themselves tend to serve as reinforcers. These memories continue to be the individual's rewards for staying in the relationship. They outweigh some of the bad points of the relationship. People sometimes stay together in bad relationships simply because they believe that the punishment they would experience in breaking up would outweigh the negatives of staying in the relationship.

Many psychologists believe that we select our friends based on reinforcement. If a friend often compliments us, that makes us feel good. We tend to want to be with them often and see them frequently. On the other hand, if a friend or an individual is not very attentive and rarely compliments us, we tend to avoid them or at least decrease the amount of time we spend with them.

This can extend to our jobs. If your job as a salesperson or sales manager is rewarding, you will tend to stay in it.

Rewards, unfortunately, do change. Financial rewards, while always good reinforcers, can eventually be taken for granted. As your needs change, so do your financial goals.

Take for example the New York Life Insurance Agency with which I consulted. The manager of this branch office made about $200,000 a year as the agency head. While he realized that it would be extremely difficult, at least in the short term, to have that kind of income in another job, he was extremely dissatisfied with his current position. The level of punishment he experienced by not running his own business outweighed the reward and reinforcement of making that much money in the agency.

So he left one of the best jobs within the New York Life Insurance Company system. His goals had changed. He wanted his own business. The job as agency manager was no longer satisfying and fulfilling because it failed to give him the rewards and reinforcers he considered important.

It is very important for us to evaluate which reinforcers are effective in our lives. Money can be a reinforcer for only some people and for only some of the time. It is extremely important to find other reinforcers as well.

PUNISHMENT

We stressed earlier that punishment should be avoided in trying to create a behavior. Punishments involve weakening a behavior by not giving an effective reinforcer or reward. If, in other words, in the process of making prospecting phone calls, you ceased to receive any appointments (rewards), it wouldn't take long before you found making the calls to be a punishing experience. Ultimately, you would stop making those phone calls.

You can also receive punishment if you have normal and natural rewards withheld. For example, an individual I know who had a beer in the evening before dinner after work found that if he couldn't have his beer (his reward), it was a punishing experience.

Punishment works extremely fast and can have side effects. Anyone who has been fired from a job or who has been reprimanded knows that punishment can cause anxiety as well as a long-term decrease in self-esteem and self-confidence. Punishing experiences can reinforce our self-sabotaging fears and limit our productivity.

Almost every cat lover knows that if a cat accidently steps on a hot stove, not only will it never step on another hot stove, it won't step on a cold stove either. In many cases, similar avoidance behavior occurs in sales when a salesperson has had a bad experience with a prospect. If the experience was punishing enough, there is a strong likelihood that the salesperson will avoid that kind of prospect in the future.

Punishment both from having a negative experience and from not receiving an expected reward can potentially destroy discipline. Motivational speakers may tell you that prospects don't reject you, they reject the product. But this does not make it any easier to accept the rejection (the punishment). Almost all of us every day feel personally rejected when someone says "no." One of the best ways to get over the punishment is to minimize the rejection's punishing effect and maximize the reward's gratifying effect.

One of the biggest problems salespeople have is that the rewards are so deferred and the rejections so immediate. For example, I consulted at a real estate company a few years ago. The manager of the company did what in my opinion was a brilliant thing. With his new salespeople, he realized that there was a better than 90 percent chance they would feel so rejected by sales calls that they would soon quit. He wanted to give these salespeople rewards that would far outweigh any punishment they would receive on the telephone prospecting for listings (individuals who wanted to sell their house through the real estate agency).

He amortized the average commission over the number of prospective client contacts it took to get a sale. He realized that each prospective client contact the new real estate agent made was worth approximately $10. So he paid them $10 for every call.

As you might have guessed, sales increased by 120% with new people, and the attrition rate dropped to only about 50%. Obviously giving them an immediate reward for a prospective client contact call was much more gratifying than the rejection was punishing.

Peak Performance Selling: How to Increase Your Sales by 70% in 6 Weeks focuses on encouraging you to determine rewards for yourself that are sufficiently gratifying and fulfilling to outweigh any punishing situation you can experience in your selling career. You can use psychological techniques to turn even the worst rejection you receive into beneficial rewards and reinforcers.

EXTINCTION

A byproduct of punishment called *extinction* can actually kill your sales career. Extinction occurs when we consistently fail to receive an expected reward. Its effect can be more far-reaching than any other form of punishment, because often we refuse to engage in that behavior ever again.

With laboratory rats that expect to receive food pellets after pressing a lever a set number of times, it has been observed that if the rat is given a food pellet after every three or four presses on the lever, it would keep pressing the lever frequently until it was satiated. When a food pellet failed to travel down the chute after the usual number of presses, this would be a punishment to the rat. In the laboratory, if the rat on a fixed reinforcement schedule of four presses did not receive a food pellet by the thirteenth press, extinction would occur—it would no longer press the lever.

The same concept holds true in sales. Numerous salespeople when presenting new products find it difficult to change styles of selling. With a new marketplace and new benefits, even experienced salespeople often meet with resistance from prospects and customers. If punishment occurs enough or if rejection occurs with a high enough frequency, extinction occurs. The salesperson refuses to sell the product at all. He has not received the usual reward of making a sale.

Individuals who leave sales sometimes do so because they are punished into extinction. In the real estate business, I frequently meet individuals who have gone into other types of selling. Recently I met a saleswoman with a major long-distance telephone company. I had first met her a year earlier when she was selling real estate. When I asked her why she quit, she simply said she didn't enjoy the career. Her sales behavior with real estate had become extinct. She'd received so much punishment that she no longer made any connection between trying to sell real estate and the rewards of generating commissions.

INCREASING ACTIVITY

While all of us have set habit patterns. and while our basic personality behavior patterns are already formed, we continually are establishing or extinguishing new habits. We are actually learning every day how to be successful or, in turn, learning slowly how to fail.

Take the basic idea of rewards and punishments that we've discussed. By giving yourself a reward after a cold call, for example, you help decrease your dislike of that business tool, the telephone, and help establish cold calling as a habit. We can take control and consciously use rewards to establish habits that we want to help us increase our own sales performance, instead of letting rewards or reinforcers randomly establish our habits.

A number of stockbrokers at a New York brokerage company I consulted with found that they had great difficulty getting used to making telephone calls in prospecting for business. One broker in particular was having an extremely difficult time making referral calls.

I wanted to find out what his rewards or reinforcers were. He told me that he especially liked hot chocolate. He usually had a cup every evening. Since he enjoyed drinking hot chocolate, we used it as a reinforcer to try to get him to make his referral phone calls. In fact, his goal was to make approximately ten referral calls each evening, which would usually give him about two booked appointments.

His behavior of making referral calls was rewarded with hot chocolate. After every call he made, he would receive a sip of hot chocolate. It was just enough to give him a nice-tasting reward, and he also felt very good about the achievement. His behavior of making referral calls increased 300 percent within a two-week period. He stayed at that level as long as I worked with that agency.

I checked back within a year, and he was still making approximately ten to twelve referral calls every single evening. This may not seem like very much, but for someone who before the program had trouble making even one referral call a day, it was a dramatic increase.

This same technique can also be used in booking appointments or even for going on appointments. Another individual I worked with had no trouble making phone calls, but did have great difficulty both qualifying and asking people for appointments.

One thing he enjoyed doing very much was playing tennis in the evening at his local tennis club. In fact, left undisciplined, he would usually go and play tennis from about 2:30 or 3 in the afternoon until 6 or 7 in the evening. We found that tennis was a very enjoyable behavior, so we linked it as a reward to his behavior of booking appointments.

His goal was to book approximately four appointments per day. He usually had a one-appointment, or 25 percent, fallout between booking and actually going on appointments. He would receive, as a reward, time playing tennis in the evening—but only after he booked his four appointments. Again, in this case, by using tennis as a reward, he increased his activity, and thereby increased his productivity and profitability 300 to 400 percent within one month.

ENJOYING PRODUCTION

Giving yourself rewards for an activity you want to increase is designed to help you enjoy the activity, whether it be making cold calls or going out on appointments.

Feeling like you are achieving your goal is nice, but since you are linking the activity, such as a cold call, which may not be very enjoyable or satisfying, with something that is highly enjoyable, such as tennis-playing or drinking hot chocolate, you may also begin to enjoy the activity you perhaps previously dreaded.

If you link such rewards with the activities you want to increase or behaviors you want to change, you will find there is no limit to the number of changes you can make in yourself—no limit to the modifications you can make to cause yourself to become not only highly profitable in business but also a happier individual in your personal life.

BUILDING DISCIPLINE—6 WEEKS TO ESTABLISHING A HABIT PATTERN

Rewards cannot only help increase activity, but can also help instill needed discipline, as well as eliminate feelings of guilt for not doing enough work, or not working fast enough. Your performance program focuses on showing you the fastest way to increase your productivity and profitability.

I'm frequently asked by individuals around the country about how long it takes to establish a habit pattern.

Well, the answer is right between three and six weeks.

If you do anything consistently for three to six weeks, you can establish a habit pattern.

As we discussed earlier, habits are extremely difficult to break. They are much more easily established.

There are good and bad sides to this. It's good because we can ward off nonproductive behaviors or habit patterns that may infect us like viruses—habits like swearing, yelling, tardiness, or even being untidy. All these habits take between three to six weeks to establish. Since it takes this long, we can't just one day fall into the habit of being late or untidy because such behavior takes about three to six weeks to become habitual.

But the time it takes to establish a habit has a bad side, mainly because it's difficult to behave as we want to for three to six weeks straight without feeling anxious or frustrated. For example, if you decide you want to start a habit of reading for about one hour every evening, you may find it very difficult to establish the habit if you forget to do that activity even one or two nights during the three to six weeks. The frustration comes from having to start over from ground zero to build the habit.

We need to do a behavior consistently for this length of time to make it really start becoming a habit. The only way I know of to establish a habit that will help you improve yourself is to use the one thing this program is dedicated to

Conditioning theory

While it only takes three to six weeks to implement a habit, something else is needed after the six-week period to maintain that habit. Something has to be used to insure that that habit stays set, like plaster of Paris.

The best example I can give for this is an experiment done by Stanford University in 1982. Stanford University did a number of projects and research on primates. In this experiment, chimpanzees were taught very simple behaviors that instilled habits. One chimpanzee was given a banana only if he pressed a lever after a light came on two times, followed by a loud buzzer. If the chimpanzee pressed the lever after the first or second light, he would not receive a reward. The only time he received a banana was when he pressed the lever after the two lights came on and the buzzer sounded.

Well this habit, as you might have guessed, was established within a three-week period. By three weeks, the chimpanzee would press the lever after the two lights and the buzzer came on, without even receiving the banana as a reward.

The habit was established; but after about another three weeks had passed without receiving a reward, the chimpanzee decided that pressing the lever wasn't worth doing, so he quit altogether because he no longer received the banana reward. To get the chimpanzee to hit the lever then, a banana was required as a reward more frequently. But the researchers decided not to give the chimpanzee a banana after every two lights and a buzzer; instead they gave him one after every tenth or twentieth time the sequence of lights and buzzer occurred.

The point is that after the three- to six-week period, when your habit is established, you don't need to give yourself consistent daily rewards anymore. But you do need to maintain your habit by giving yourself an occasional reward, such as a weekend trip, extra television time if you enjoy it, or even more time playing tennis. In this way, you can help maintain and solidfy that habit.

A good illustration here is of a mother whose son swore incessantly. The son swore so badly, in fact, that the mother felt very embarrassed taking him anywhere in public. The 10-year-old was put on a conditioning program in which she tried to develop in him a habit of not swearing or a habit of keeping a clean mouth. To do this, the mother gave the son 25 cents every evening, or $1.75 a week, for not using any swear words.

After a five-week period, because of the rewards, the son did not swear at all. Note that he was rewarded for keeping a clean mouth and not punished for swearing. She totally cut out the 25-cent rewards after the five-week period. The son started swearing every once in a while after about two months. She then gave the son, randomly, 25 cents on days that he did not swear. She kept it random so that the son never knew on what day he would be rewarded with the 25 cents.

Along with this, the mother didn't buy the son toys. She also didn't buy the son candy. The son was required to earn his own money. The son began to feel that he shouldn't swear, but should have as clean a mouth as possible, because this was an easy way to earn 25 cents.

MAINTAINING BEHAVIORS

Behaviors do need to be maintained, through reinforcement, at least infrequently, and this is really the same idea the slot machine is based on. If a slot machine gave you money every time you pulled the handle, you would probably keep putting quarters in and pulling the handle until you dropped from exhaustion.

But a slot machine is designed to maintain your habit of pulling the "arm" or handle and putting quarters in by rewarding you, not every time you pull the handle, but infrequently—maybe every tenth, twentieth, or thirtieth time. This is the casino's way of making sure you maintain your established habit of gambling, using the slot machines.

This is the premise that gambling is based on. You are rewarded by the casino just enough to keep you playing, but not enough to let everyone win big or win heavily. At the same time, if you lost money every single time you played, you probably wouldn't gamble. They let you win enough so you feel you are rewarded for gambling once in a while.

Habits you form and reinforce this way are also the hardest to break.

As we discussed earlier, these are called intermittent rewards, or variable ratio reinforcements, because you are variably, or randomly, rewarded for activities.

In chapters 16 and 17, you can learn more about how to develop your own conditioning program to change your behaviors and increase your sales production.

16

The Peak Performance Technique: Incremental Sales Production versus Successive Approximation

After you read this book and apply the concepts we talk about, you will probably find yourself doing a lot more of the high-priority things you previously put off doing or avoided altogether.

You will likely find yourself becoming much more productive.

You are also likely to find yourself making more money, getting closer and closer to realizing your goals, having probably two or three times as much business.

Unfortunately, you'll also find yourself encountering stress as a result of the changes brought about by having more business. Stress results from changes that bring on psychological and physical problems.

THE PSYCHOLOGY OF CHANGE

In figure 16.1, labeled "Psychology of Change," you will find a graphic model which shows a comfort zone in the middle, bordered on the top by anxiety and on the bottom by depression.

You have probably been to a lecture sometime when a motivational speaker said, especially if you are a salesperson, that if you make twenty calls every single day, you'll be a millionaire in the next two weeks. So you take the speaker up on the advice and make twenty calls. The next day you make 14 calls, the next day you make ten calls, the fourth day you make five calls, and the fifth day the only call you make is to your mother, and you talk with her all day long.

Questions going through most managers' and salespeoples' heads nowadays are like this: "Why can't I maintain the high level of activity I want?"

Undoubtedly, you make more money if you're active. "Why do I have business fluctuations? Why am I not making as much money now as I was making eighteen months ago? Or even one year ago?"

The answer to these questions lies in a very simple thing called the *comfort zone theory*. Whatever you are doing in terms of activity right now is called your comfort zone. You feel good at that level, you probably feel comfortable, but, more important, it's a level at which you find yourself experiencing no dissonance or distress—at least not enough to change.

As soon as you increase your activity, you experience that one thing which you probably dread, *anxiety*. Indications of anxiety are when you

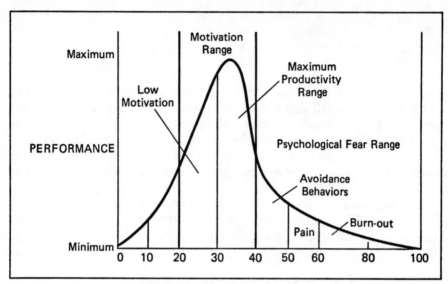

Figure 16.1. Psychology of Change

begin to feel worried when you are making those twenty phone calls. You feel pressured, pushed. The world is closing in around you; you suddenly have no time; everybody is demanding things of you. Anxiety and distress set in, causing you to drop right back down to the comfort zone with a lower activity level.

One of the prime reasons New Year's resolutions don't work is that they require too much of a change all at once. A few years ago, I promised myself I would read one book a day. I once was a very fast reader—about 5,000 to 6,000 words a minute—but the change in my reading behavior, going from one-half hour to ninety minutes of reading per day, caused anxiety because of the extra activity. It wasn't long—about a month—before I dropped right back to my comfort zone of reading only about two or three chapters per night during my usual one-half hour.

The experience called *depression* is indicated graphically at the bottom of figure 16.1.

What if you did nothing during the day?
What if you just showed up at work?
What if you just filed papers or talked to fellow employees?

Because you purchased this book, you are probably a highly moti-vated individual. When you do nothing productive, you probably start feeling guilty. But you probably can't meet your own expectations of how much you should accomplish during the day. You probably are upset at yourself for not achieving more during the day.

You most likely are an individual who plainly feels good when you can look back and say, "I accomplished something today; I did something worthwhile."

For you, doing nothing probably promotes depression, lack of motivation, lethargy, as well as feelings of worthlessness, low self-esteem, and low self-confidence. Since you don't like feeling depressed, you jump right back into your comfort zone.

There are actually two ways to achieve your desired change and cope with the anxiety the extra activity produces in you. The first is that while you're trying to change something in your life—whether it be increasing phone calls, the number of people you see, or even the number of pages you read, or your weight loss—make sure you don't increase your activity too fast. Do it slowly, so you'll be assured of maintaining that activity. This will help you modify your productivity and change, but, more important, it will help keep you changed.

By using the very simple conditioning techniques we've already discussed, you can really do anything you want to do. But just make sure that, if you are a salesperson, you do not try to go too quickly from making five phone calls—which may be in your comfort zone—up to making twenty phone calls. Make sure you increase the number perhaps two phone calls every three days, until you bring yourself up to twenty phone calls after about four to five weeks, thus avoiding a sudden change that might promote stress.

USING SUDS

The second way to manage change is to make sure that every single day—whether or not you are keeping track of your SUDS (Subjective Unit of Discomfort Scale, see chapter 8, figure 8.1) level or doing the progressive relaxation techniques (see chapter 8) for 90 seconds when your SUDS level is too high—*you take one-half hour in total solitude to totally and absolutely relax.*

This will help you experience less stress on your road to productivity.

KEEP YOUR MIND ON WHAT YOU WANT

Many people I talk to, when I ask them why they aren't making more money, respond, "Well, I just don't want to work that hard."

The Peak Performance Technique

The big problem, I'm sure, is not that they don't want to work that hard, but that they don't want to experience the stress that high activity would bring them. Please, try to realize that your activity and your quest for the goal by the date that you want it will bring you anxiety and stress if you work too hard too fast. It will bring you stress if you don't use the stress-coping techniques I have suggested—including the progressive relaxation technique.

Pace yourself. Don't shoot for the moon within two days and expect to reach it. Work towards it gradually, and you will be assured of gaining anything you could possibly want, and, more important, be happy with it.

Years ago, when I was watching a newscast, I saw that George Foreman was about to fight Muhammad Ali. The interviewer, obviously not knowing or feeling much for boxing, asked George a question: "George, you're a guy who's been hit in the face thousands of times, but you still go back for more. How do you do it, George?"

I thought about that, "My gosh! think of it—getting hit in the face for a living!"

And George Foreman answered, "When I think real hard about what I want, I don't feel the pain. When I think real hard about knocking out my opponent, I don't feel getting hit, I don't feel headaches, I don't feel anything. And all I think about and taste and hear and see is knocking out and winning the boxing match."

One of the most profound things that I ever heard came from a man who was a ninth-grade dropout. George Foreman said something that struck me hard, and it really all boils down to the idea that when you concentrate on what you want, you don't feel the sacrifice. When you think hard about what you desire, it doesn't seem like such hard work.

In the late 1970s, I got a chance to play some of the greatest tennis pros in the world. When I was on the European Grand Prix Tour, I got a chance to play in Austria, against the national champion from Rumania. Besides being a great player, he also was a bit intimidating.

In one match against him, I remember I was feeling a bit nervous playing him, but I was holding my own. Well, something snapped in the second set of a three-set match. I found myself only partially effective. I found myself only getting in about twenty percent of my first serves. In tennis, the first serve is the key. If you can get your first serve in, you can keep pressure on your opponent, and if you put pressure on your opponent you cause him to make mistakes. Well, twenty percent accuracy on my first serve was not helping. In fact, it was a great hindrance. I found myself gradually losing the set.

In between games, I went over to the sideline and I had a drink of water. I suddenly remembered a book that I had read a few years earlier called *The Inner Game of Tennis.* This book, written by Tim Galway, was an extremely innovative tennis book, centered on using mind control. I immediately understood that I wasn't concentrating on where I wanted the serve to go. I was only focusing on trying to hit the ball in good tennis form and style. That was causing my downfall because I was concentrating on details of my service stroke instead of on what I wanted the serve to do.

Well, I took Galway's advice and started concentrating on the exact spot where I wanted to hit the serve, instead of whether I had my elbow high or whether I was reaching up for the ball. All I could think about, as I threw that ball up to serve, was the exact spot—a minute particle on the court, the area on the service court on the Rumanian's backhand side, the exact place where I wanted the ball to go after I served. And, as if something magical happened, every ball I served went to the spot I concentrated on. When I took my mind off details—the distracting little things in my stroke—and started concentrating on what I wanted, the ball started landing right every time.

The bottom line is this

If you can focus on what you want and not get caught up in details, if you can think about your goals and not think about the difficulty in achieving them, you'll meet with success you've never experienced before, without feeling a great deal of pain in the effort.

In my experience, most people fear work that goes into achieving things because much of this work is full of painful struggle and stress. They have to work harder, therefore they feel more anxiety.

USING REWARDS

During the discussion on conditioning techniques, you learned why rewards are really the only means of establishing a behavior or a habit pattern. If, as a child, you got an ice-cream cone for putting your bike away, it wouldn't be long before you automatically put your bike away. Or perhaps your mother gave you 25 cents every time you helped do the dishes. You probably did the dishes or did something to help her almost every evening until you grew tired of receiving the money as a reward.

To properly help yourself change your habit patterns or increase your productivity, you should give yourself a reward for the things that you want to change.

REWARDS AND REINFORCERS

Look at figure 16.2, titled "Rewards and Reinforcers." On it a number of different rewards are indicated, ranging from bubblebaths to anything

√	Activities	Impor-tance	Measure-ment	Frequency
	Watching television			
	Listening to the radio			
	Cup of coffee, tea			
	Being alone			
	Reading newspaper, magazine, book			
	Exercise--jogging, spa, aerobics			
	Hobby			
	Long baths or bubble bath			
	Eating favorite foods			
	Going to movie, play, concert			
	Sports--tennis skiing, swimming			
	Going out for dinner			
	Smoking			

Activity Checklist: Check the activities you do, whether or not you enjoy them.
Importance: On a 1-to-10 scale, how enjoyable, how important is this activity
(not necessarily in relation to the others checked)?
Measurement: When you engage in this activity, how much time do you usually spend?
How much do you eat or drink? How many? (e.g., 2 hours, one-hour, 1 cup or glass,
1 magazine, 1 apple, etc.)
Frequency: How often do you do this activity? (e.g., each day, twice per day, once
a week, once a month, etc.)

Figure 16.2. Rewards and Reinforcers

you'd like to write in at the bottom of the sheet. Make a copy of this sheet so you can include it in the file or notebook you use as your productivity notebook.

To determine what rewards you find most reinforcing, put a check mark next to everything you do that's named in the Rewards and Reinforcers list, whether or not you enjoy doing it.

Under the category marked "importance," rate each item you check on a 1-to-10 scale (1 is low; 10 is high) according to how enjoyable each of these activities is.

How important is it?

How committed are you to doing it?

Rewards and Reinforcers

The next category is "time spent." When you do each of these things, how long do you spend doing it or how much do you do it? For example, if you marked down "sports," indicate the number of hours spent playing when you do play, whereas drinking coffee would be expressed in number of cups per day.

Next is "frequency."

How often do you do it? Several times each day? Once a day? Once a week?

Mark this down. The information here that you include in your tailor-made productivity workbook can help you better use your favorite pastimes as rewards to change your own habit patterns.

17

The 6-Week Technique: Matching Activity Levels and Rewards to the Six-Week Format

BEHAVIORAL CONTRACTS

Society has imposed ways to get us to commit to or take responsibility for our actions. Society has even found a way to help prevent us from making mistakes. These techniques or mechanisms society controls us by are called *contracts*.

Contracts are really agreements that are such a part of our lives that virtually every man, woman, and child in the United States is under one. In many agreements we enter into, we commit ourselves to keep our word by signing something that we call a contract.

In this chapter on behavioral contracts, you will find information on ways to control yourself so you can accomplish virtually anything you want. You'll also discover ways to reward yourself for activities or behaviors you want to develop in yourself, which in turn will serve to double or even quadruple your income *within six- to eight-weeks*.

If you successfully complete your six- to eight-week behavioral contract—which is extremely simple to carry out—you will find that your productivity, as well as your overall enjoyment and achievement, will skyrocket.

The behavioral contract we discuss in this chapter is really a promise or agreement you will make to yourself (you'll ideally involve another person as your productivity partner) to change yourself or implement changes on a regular basis to literally and absolutely increase your overall performance. The contract is organized so you can change yourself temporarily, as well as permanently, into the person you want to be—to be financially more profitable or to help yourself make as much as you're prepared to make.

CREATING YOUR OWN BEHAVIORAL CONTRACT

Look at figures 17.1 through 17.3, titled, "Behavioral Contracts." On these sheets there are a number of categories; on the top is something titled, "If" and "Then."

BEHAVIORAL CONTRACT

EFFECTIVE DATES: From July 9, 1987 To August 22, 1903

IF I make 3 contacts each day THEN I will receive 1 token after each call and TV time that night.

IF I book 1 appointment each day THEN I will receive 1 cup of coffee after I book the appointment and can read my favorite book.

IF I go on 1 appointment each day THEN I can play tennis in the evening or see a friend on the way home.

BONUS: If I achieve my goal each and every day for the week for contacts, booked appointments, and face to face appointments, then my wife and I can go out to dinner at the restaurant of my choice.

CONTROL: My wife will meet with me every day to discuss my goal activity and help me keep track. I will give $100 to my wife for security. If I give myself a reward without earning it, or fall off the program before 6 weeks are completed, she may spend the $100 as she pleases.

_____
Goal Achiever

_____
Partner

This contract will be reviewed on _____
date

Figure 17.1. Behavioral Contract–Sales

BEHAVIORAL CONTRACT

EFFECTIVE DATES: From _____July 9, 1987_____ To _____August 22, 1987_____

IF _Johnny picks up any of his_
toys, clothes, etc. in his
room...

THEN _I will give him one_
army man immediately and
praise him.

IF _Johnny is well-behaved_
during the day and does what
he is told upon first
request....

THEN _I will give him 50¢_
just before he goes to bed
and praise him during the
day.

IF _____

THEN _____

BONUS: _If Johnny succeeds in picking up each day and being_
well- behaved all week and earns his rewards each day, then
I will take him to the play area of his choice for 1 hour or
more on the weekend; e.g., park, beach, etc.

CONTROL: _I will deposit $100 with my spouse which will be_
refunded if I complete the 6-week program with Johnny and if I
give Johnny the rewards when he has earned them. I promise to
meet with my spouse daily to review Johnny's target behavior
activity and his attitude.

_____

Goal Achiever

_____

Partner

This contract will be reviewed on _____
date

Figure 17.2. Behavioral Contract–Child's Behavior

BEHAVIORAL CONTRACT

EFFECTIVE DATES: From _____ To _____

IF _____   THEN _____
_____   _____
_____   _____
_____   _____

IF _____   THEN _____
_____   _____
_____   _____
_____   _____

IF _____   THEN _____
_____   _____
_____   _____
_____   _____

BONUS: _____
_____
_____
_____

CONTROL: _____
_____
_____
_____
_____
_____

_____
Goal Achiever

_____
Partner

This contract will be reviewed on _____
                                        date

Figure 17.3. Behavioral Contract

THE "IF" COLUMN

The "If" column represents the target behaviors you want to develop. For example, in figure 17.1, making more referral calls or making more appointments and in figure 17.2, gaining a child's cooperation are the target behaviors. Figure 17.3 is a blank sheet you can use as a model for your own behavioral contract to reach your desired target behavior. Make a copy of your behavioral contract and include it in your productivity file or notebook.

Fill this "If" section in with statements such as "If I make six cold calls each day . . . ," or "If I book one appointment per day . . . ," or "If Johnny puts his toys away . . .".

Record each step you have planned.

THE "THEN" COLUMN

The "Then" statements denote the reward you will give yourself for changing your behavior, or, in some cases, the reward someone else will give you. The "Then" becomes a consequence only of making a change—of fulfilling the "If" statement.

Opposite an example of an "If" statement such as "If I make five phone calls each day . . . ," you might write, ". . . Then I can watch the evening news."

"If Johnny puts his toys away each evening . . . ," "Then I will give him 25 cents."

The "Then" part of the contract can be drawn from your "Rewards and Reinforcers" sheet (figure 16.2). Any reward can be used if you've rated it an enjoyment level of at least 6. It's something you should give yourself if you earn it—but not before you earn it.

Rewards do and will work to increase your performance but only if you use them as directed in the program. Link the reward directly to the target behavior—don't defer your reward any more than a few hours. For example, you wouldn't link the reward of golf to a daily increase in referral calls, since you probably can't golf every day. However, golf could be a weekly bonus.

THE "BONUS" COLUMN

Directly beneath the "If" and "Then" columns is something labeled "Bonus." The "Bonus" is a reward for successfully accomplishing the *weekly* goals and activities you set for yourself. This bonus can be something like giving yourself a dinner at a nice restaurant on Saturday night after completing a week's goals. Anything you think would be rewarding would help reinforce your motivation to accomplish goals during the week, thereby increasing your productivity.

YOUR PRODUCTIVITY PARTNER

Directly below the bonus section, write in the name of your "productivity partner." Choose somebody—ideally a spouse or someone you work with and trust—who can help you enforce this contract and encourage you throughout the six- to eight-week program you are embarking upon to change your habits. This individual should be someone you see daily—someone who can discuss your goals and accomplishments with you, someone who can commit to being supportive of your efforts for at least six to eight weeks.

Since often we may rationalize ourselves into giving ourselves a reward even when we haven't earned it, a partner is not only a good idea but is truly necessary to help keep you on track to change the things you want to change.

Along with finding a partner to help keep you on track, you should be prepared to do one more thing. To further help keep you committed to this program,

write a check to your partner for $100 or more.

If you fall short of your contractual obligations, if you fail to give yourself a designated reward, or if you decide before the six- to eight-week termination point that you want to quit this program for any reason except changing your goals, you forfeit the $100 to your partner. If you quit before the six- to eight-week period is up, you should tell your partner to cash the check without your permission and spend it any way he or she sees fit.

While this is a difficult commitment to make, if you do sincerely want to change and to commit yourself to making more money or achieving your goal by your target date, this is a small price to pay to help keep yourself committed.

DEFINING YOUR GOALS

Now select the goal you wish to start working toward during the next six to eight weeks. If it is a major goal, like making $100,000 a year, break it down into segments so you know exactly how much work you need to do to make steady progress every month, every week, and, if you can determine, every day.

For example, on the goal of making $100,000, divide it by twelve. This will tell you the amount you need to make each month—around $8,500. If you break it down further, you need to make about $2,000 a week; and you can even break that down to a daily target, if you like.

CONTRACTING TO GET YOUR GOALS

A computer accessories salesman whom I worked with for a six- to eight-week program had this goal: a Pearson 31-foot yacht. The yacht cost approximately $50,000. The salesman earned only about $2,000 a month. He sold around two products a week—eight products a month—and his average commission was approximately $250, so you can see that it would be difficult, at best, for him to buy a yacht outright or even to lease it.

He also set a goal for himself to purchase that yacht within two months. Now, since his goal depended on him generating a larger income, he needed to increase the number of products he sold.

His averages dictated that to get one sale, he must see about two prospects; to see two prospects, he must book about three appointments; to book three appointments, he needed to call, on a referral basis, ten people. His average activity showed that he was calling on referral basis approximately twenty people a week. He was booking about six appointments a week and seeing about two prospects a week, which yielded him two sales per week, for a weekly grand total of $500.

The lease on the yacht would cost him around $600 a month. For this salesperson, that meant generating about three more sales per month. This translated into calling thirty more referrals per month, or almost eight more referrals a week. He would also have to book nine more appointments and see six more prospects per month. This would have to be done over and beyond the number of sales he needed to maintain his standard of living.

So you see, to start leasing the yacht on the date he wanted, he would only have to work a little harder to increase his activity. If this seems to you like a lot more work, keep in mind *the law of forced efficiency* which holds that if you push yourself to do something, you'll always find an easier way to do it. In this particular example, this salesperson, when faced with making more calls, found easier ways to make referral calls and tended to qualify the people he was prospecting much more effectively. Eventually he wasn't doing that much more activity, he was just improving his efficiency and, as a result, his productivity. He wasn't working more; he was just working smarter.

The way we started this individual on the program was very simple. We knew he was currently making, in terms of activity, around four referral calls per day, booking about one appointment per day, and seeing around one prospect per day. He was also making one sale, on the average, every two days.

Although he ultimately would have to increase his activity, we started him at his current normal activity level, to try to get him used to the program. His Rewards and Reinforcers sheet indicated he enjoyed, on an importance level of 6 or more, watching television, playing tennis, and drinking coffee. He also enjoyed going out to dinner on the weekends.

The coffee-drinking was linked to calls. For every call he made, he could take a sip or drink of his coffee. If he made no phone calls, he received no coffee that day. Since he also liked to watch television in the evening, we linked television time—about an hour—to appointments, so if he went on an appointment, he could watch one hour of television. No appointments that day, no television.

The last reward we linked to an activity was tennis. Since this individual greatly enjoyed playing tennis, but only a couple of times a week, we linked seeing prospects to playing tennis, so for every two prospects he saw (usually he saw two a day), he would receive an afternoon or evening of playing tennis.

There was no reward given for the number of sales he made, because basically, if his activities increased, we knew sales would follow. No salesperson will be active or increase activity for very long without having sales go up a proportional amount.

The bonus for this salesman was that if he accomplished his goals for the week—namely, making four referral calls per day, booking one appointment per day, and seeing one prospect per day—he could go out to a nice restaurant and have a wonderful dinner as a reward.

The second week with this individual, he increased his phone calls by one call per day. It wasn't until the fourth week that he also increased his booked appointments, as well as the number of prospects he saw during the day.

By making a slow, steady increase, he was able to adjust to the extra activity, preventing stress and strain. He also adjusted to rewarding himself or not giving himself rewards, depending on the activity he performed.

In this example, by the eighth week, he had approximately tripled the number of sales he was making because he tripled the amount of activity he was doing before sales. It didn't take him long to triple his sales—and without working any harder. He just learned to work smarter and better.

In another case, I worked with a manager who didn't make phone calls but found he either did not take the time or didn't have the time to read more business-related articles and books. His target behavior was to spend more time reading, thereby increasing his efficiency in his job. His goal was to read about two extra books per month. In breaking that down, he needed to read about ten more pages, or one chapter, per day.

He saw numerous benefits to his peak performance program

He could get more information which made him more valuable to the company.

He was also in a good position to directly increase his pay because of the new skills he was picking up through the extra reading.

He also found that his job became more interesting because he was gaining more information from his reading.

We started this manager off by putting him on a very simple program in which we tried to get him to read one more page per day. It usually took him only about one to two minutes, but just getting the book out, looking at the page and reading it was enough to start a habit pattern of reading.

In time we would increase that. But more important at first was just getting a book in front of him.

We found from his Rewards and Reinforcers sheet that he enjoyed walking around the block at noon. Walking, on his "Importance Scale," was an 8. Every time he read one page, he could have his noon walk.

After the third and fourth week, he was awarded with a walk for every five pages. By increasing him slowly, it was around six weeks before he was actually reading ten pages or one chapter per day. If he met his reading goals each of the five workdays, his bonus was that he could play eighteen holes of golf.

A final example of how to arrange behavioral contracts involves the case of a real estate salesperson. This realtor's goal was to be able to buy a house by the end of a twelve-month period. The house had a $1,000 monthly mortgage. For this, along with other goals like extra spending money and new clothes, she needed to sell one more house every month, which would give her an extra $1,000 commission. Since only one out of every two escrows she opened actually closed, she really needed to sell two extra houses per month to close one extra escrow per month.

Her averages showed that to close one sale she needed to show eight houses. To show eight houses, she needed to book sixteen appointments, because of high fallout. To book sixteen appointments, she needed to make 160 phone calls per month.

On a weekly basis, this proved very simple indeed. Since she needed to sell one more house per month, she needed to go on two more showings per week, to book four more appointments per week, and to make around forty more referral calls per week; this came out to eight calls per day, one booked appointment per day, and one showing every two days.

On a daily basis, this seemed less work than she anticipated. In other words, she really needed to double her activity so she could afford to buy the house within one year. Again, I started her off with present work levels, not wanting to increase her effort too quickly for fear that she would become upset, stressed, and anxious by a sudden increase in her activity.

Her Rewards and Reinforcers sheet indicated she smoked cigarettes, which she rated a 7. She also enjoyed seeing friends in the evening, which she rated a 7. She also enjoyed jogging, and rated that an 8.

She was put on a program whereby she could smoke one cigarette after she made one referral call. She smoked ten cigarettes per day, so after the eighth call—her goal for the day—she could smoke as many as she wanted.

Since she also enjoyed jogging on a daily basis, she was rewarded with jogging in the evening if and only if she booked one appointment to show a house that day. Since she enjoyed seeing friends and rated that a 7, every time she showed a house, she would reward herself with a visit to a friend. Since she only showed a house every two days, this rewarded her with frequent visits to friends—but only if she first showed a property.

In this case as with others, she wasn't required to increase her activity very quickly. It was done on a slow and methodical basis, so after around six weeks, her activity had reached the point where she was, based on her averages, selling one extra house per month and putting herself well on track to reaching her twelve-month goal of buying a new house with a $1,000 monthly mortgage.

KNOW YOUR AVERAGES

Now, take the time to write down your own averages. If you're unsure how to do this, please refer to chapters 11 and 12 on averages or to figures 17.4 and 17.5:

KNOWING YOUR WEEKLY ACTIVITY

Please also write down your current weekly and daily activity in a log and compare this to your target behavior (see figures 17.6 through 17.9).

WHAT ARE YOUR AVERAGES?

1 SALE = _____ # APPTS = _____ # BOOKED APPTS = _____ # CALLS

OR 1 SALE = WHAT TARGET ACTIVITY

FOR EXAMPLE: 1 SALE = 3 APPTS = 4 BOOKED APPTS = 40 CALLS
                        1 SALE = 40 CALLS
            IF   1 SALE = $800 COMMISSION, THEN 1 CALL = $20

Figure 17.4. What Are Your Averages?

Finally, break down your goal and decide how much more activity you will need to achieve your objective by the date you have specified. Next, start linking the rewards or reinforcers to each target behavior you would like to achieve.

You should now have a good idea of how fast and when to increase your activity—for example, the number of calls and appointments—so you can reach whatever target behavior and deadline you've set.

PACE YOURSELF

Frequently, individuals on this program say to me, "Kerry, I'm only making two phone calls a day now, and I'm going on about one appointment a

---

CURRENT ACTIVITY

What are you currently doing each day and week to get your goal?

Sales/week or day _____   # Appts/week or day _____

Booked appts/week or day _____   # Calls/week or day _____

OTHER TARGET BEHAVIORS
1.   Tardiness: How often are you late (or on time)?
2.   Reading: How many pages are you currently reading each day/week?
3.   How often does your child misbehave? How often does your child follow instructions?
4.   How many pounds do you want to lose?

Figure 17.5. Current Activity

WEEKLY ACTIVITY LOG

	Client	Appt Booked	Appt Kept	Contacts
Sunday				
Monday	Don Morris 237-1120	x		
	Tim Donaldson 426-1181	x		x x x x x
	Donna Blake 847-2222	x		
Tuesday	Fred James 827-1052	x		
	Tom Jana 811-1361	x		x x x x x
	Tim Parker 832-2136		x	x x
	Steve Jamison 831-2922		x	
Wednesday	Jim Jones 840-2722	x		
	Tom Linwood 832-0100	x		x x x x x
	Dick Lester 640-1237	x		x x x
	Donna Blake 847-222		x	x x x x
	Tim Donaldson 426-1181		x	
Thursday	Fred Perkins 640-1962	x		x x x x x
	John Fredricks 840-1962	x		x x x x x
	Janet Edwards 638-4026	x		x x x
	Fred James 827-1052		x	
	Tom Jana 811-1361		x	
Friday	Fritz Perry 744-7377	x		x x x x x
	Tom Montgomery 882-6449	x		x x x x
	Frank Thompson 540-6266	x		x
	Tom Linwood 837-1011		x	
Saturday				

1. Each time you make a call, put an "x" under "Contracts."
2. Each time you book an appointment, put an "x" under "Appt. Booked" with name, phone number, time and date booked.
3. Each time you actually go on an appointment, put an "x" under "Appt. Kept" with name, phone number, and time and date completed.

Figure 17.6. Weekly Activity Sheet–Sales

WEEKLY ACTIVITY LOG

	CHILD'S TARGET BEHAVIOR: PICK UP TOYS	NUMBER OF TIMES	GOAL ACHIEVED	REWARD GIVEN
Sunday				
Monday	Picked up blanket	x	yes	yes
Tuesday	Picked up books, papers, blankets	x x x	yes	yes
Wednesday	Without my asking, John picked up books, blankets and clothes	x x x x	yes	Yes!
Thursday	Didn't pick up anything even when asked		no	no
Friday	Without my asking, again he picked up all toys, clothes/ room very neat	x x x	yes	yes
Saturday	Picked up everything	x x x x x x	yes	yes

Figure 17.7. Weekly Activity Sheet–Child's Behavior

WEEKLY ACTIVITY LOG

	TITLE OF BOOK	GOAL (# PAGES)	# PAGES READ	REWARD RECEIVED
Sunday				
	See You At The Top	2	2	yes
Monday				
	See You At The Top	3	3	yes
	Spike	5	5	
Tuesday				
	See you at the top	6	0	no
	Spike	6	6	
Wednesday				
	See You At The Top	7	7	yes
	Spike	7	7	
Thursday				
	See You At the Top	10	10	yes
	Spike	10	10	
Friday				
	See You At The Top	14	14	yes
	Spike	14	14	
Saturday				

Figure 17.8. Weekly Activity Sheet–Reading

WEEKLY ACTIVITY LOG

	Activities			
Sunday				
Monday				
Tuesday				
Wednesday				
Thursday				
Friday				
Saturday				

Figure 17.9. Weekly Activity Sheet

day, but my objective is to make twenty phone calls. I'll just do that tomorrow."

This is exactly what happens at New Year's resolution time, when you promise, for example, that starting on January 2 you'll stop smoking. Then all of a sudden you realize it's August and you're still smoking more than ever. Or some people make New Year's promises to themselves to make more phone calls or go on more appointments, yet nothing ever changes.

The real reason for this is that you may expect too much of yourself too quickly, and you may think you can instantly change habit patterns by will power only. This is a basic fallacy many Americans have nowadays.

The truth is, however, that you need to have a systematic program by which you can change gradually; without such a program, you may never see improvement or change.

I do encourage you to increase your activity after your first week or so of taking reinforcers or as soon as you feel comfortable with the program. The idea, however, is to start at your present levels of activity. Ask yourself, *What level am I achieving right now?* Start at that level for about a week or two until you get used to the program and to maintaining the same amount of activity, and then increase your activity.

For example, I worked with a car salesperson who was very excited about reaching her goals within one year. She started out on this program at her present activity levels—meeting with about three people and making five referral phone calls per day. In turn, she was giving herself one piece of candy for every referral call she made, and around one half-hour of television for every appointment she went on. She kept herself at this five-call-three-appointment phase for about two weeks, even though it was not a change from her normal activity. She gave herself a chance to adapt to accepting the rewards and being on the program. Over the next two to three weeks, as she felt more comfortable with the rewards and the program, she started increasing her activity to six phone calls and four appointments per day; then seven phone calls; and then eight phone calls and five appointments a day.

Don't push yourself too hard too fast at the beginning of this program. Make sure you are totally comfortable with giving yourself rewards, and that you do give yourself a reward when you have earned it.

One of the most important concepts of this program is that *when you've earned a reward, you must take it*. If you don't give yourself a reward when you've earned it, the likelihood you'll achieve your objectives by the date that you want is very low.

SUCCESSIVE APPROXIMATION

The concept behind not increasing your activity level too quickly but changing your behavior a little at a time, is called *successive approximation*. We use successive approximation to learn to do things or to overcome fears. For example, if you have a fear of elevators, a psychologist wouldn't take you up to the top floor and say, "Look at what I did for you—you're cured," while you're on the elevator floor screaming, crying, and pounding the walls. What the psychologist would usually do on the first day is take you up to the steps that lead to the elevator, and then back. The second day, you'd both go up to the elevator door, then stop, and go home. The third day, you'd both go inside the elevator, but not up or down in it. On the fourth day, you'd both go only one floor, and then continue until you became comfortable with the elevator.

At the same time, every time your anxiety increased—and therefore your SUDS level (see chapter 8) went up, too—in response to being close to or on the elevator, the psychologist would help you relax. He or she would ask you to take three or four deep breaths as you gradually eliminated your elevator phobia.

With this program, working a little at a time towards your goal will be much more effective than trying to do too much too fast.

YOUR BONUS—THAT CERTAIN SOMETHING EXTRA

Now look at the bonus column on the behavioral contracts in figures 17.1 through 17.3. This bonus column is really meant to give you something extra—an extra reward for accomplishing what you set out to do that week. For example, if your objective was to make five referral phone calls per day and one appointment per day, and if you did make twenty-five calls and five appointments that week, then you could give yourself a nice bonus on the weekend. Perhaps going out to dinner with your spouse or taking the whole day off and just going golfing.

Obviously, if you didn't accomplish all the goals you set out to do, you couldn't take the bonus of dinner with your spouse, and you couldn't go golfing either.

You cannot take the bonus if you don't earn it. Only if you deserve a reward can you take it. By all means, make sure the bonus is something you really want. If going out to dinner is something that only your spouse wants to do, and you're just going along with the idea, it won't work. You are only trying to satisfy someone else's desires and not yours. After all, this is *your* program.

THE IMPORTANCE OF YOUR PEAK PERFORMANCE PARTNER

As I pointed out earlier in the chapter, it's also a good idea to give your performance partner a check for $100, $200, or even $300—whatever would hurt the most but would not be financially burdensome. This is only a deposit, which would be refunded to you only after you successfully complete the program. This deposit will also help ensure that you

1. Do take a reward when you deserve one.
2. Never give yourself a reward if you do not deserve one.
3. Stay on the program for at least six to eight weeks until you *do* dramatically increase your productivity and activity—which will happen.

In the control column, you should promise to interact with your partner—whether an office mate or your spouse—about your progress on the program at least once a day; you should also promise to complete a daily and weekly activity sheet, like the ones shown in figures 17.6 through 17.9. Figure 17.9 is a blank weekly activity sheet for you to use as a model and include in the file or notebook you use as your sales performance workbook. The weekly activity sheet will enable your partner to see how you have been doing.

Your partner is really your police officer. This is the individual you've designated to monitor and be supportive of your efforts to reach the goals you've scheduled for yourself.

By filling out a "Weekly/Daily Activity Sheet," you're keeping a log of what you do each day and each week, as well as giving your partner a chance to see what your activity has been. You can also use the sheet to decide whether or not you've earned a reward.

REMEMBER TO REWARD YOURSELF

We can't stress enough how important it is to take a reward when you've earned one. It is important to watch television if you earned it by making phone calls or by reading a certain number of pages you've scheduled for yourself that day.

More important, however, is making sure you get immediate rewards. A deferred reward is something like getting paid a salary every two weeks, while an immediate reward is getting something immediately, such as praise. Immediate rewards help you increase your activity much faster.

Many individuals I've worked with have given themselves a glass or half-glass of fruit juice for every phone call they make. Or they give themselves a candy bar, a bite of a candy bar, or maybe a couple of nuts for every phone call they make.

Every parent in America should know, when toilet training a child, that praise is important when the child begins to use the toilet correctly. But one thing that works even better than praise is giving the child a reward like "M&Ms." Amazingly, when children receive rewards like this for simple things like toilet training, they can't wait to get back to the toilet. You can cut in half the time it takes to toilet train a child. It usually takes anywhere from three weeks to ten months to toilet train. But parents who give immediate reward like M&Ms after the child uses the toilet, many times toilet train in two weeks or sometimes less.

Give yourself an immediate reward after you do your target behavior. Whether it be eating a piece of candy, drinking a sip of juice, or even taking a break to talk to a friend, I encourage you to take these immediate rewards every time you do the target behavior.

USING TOKENS

Another way to use an immediate reward to increase your activity or increase your target behavior is using something called *tokens*. Many times you can't eat a piece of candy after every phone call. Sometimes you make twenty calls and you'd probably make yourself sick eating candy each time. Or maybe sometimes you may not feel like drinking orange juice or taking a bite of an apple.

Tokens work equally well to give you an immediate reward, at times when you don't want your usual reward. Tokens are one of the best ways to reinforce behavior, because you can give yourself one token even when you're not hungry or thirsty for your reward.

Tokens can be used anytime, anywhere. They can be such things as poker chips, pennies, or even paper clips. Tokens are rewards you can use in two ways

1. You can, on your behavioral contract, put down that you will receive one token for every phone call that you make, or one token for every

time you ask for a referral. Each token might represent one half-hour of television time or a cup of coffee.

For every five tokens, you might receive tennis time, or even an hour of playing golf in the evening. For every ten tokens, for example, you might receive time reading your favorite pleasure book in the evening.

2. You can also use tokens by themselves to help effectively change your behavior into exactly what you want it to be. If you are working on making yourself more assertive with your prospects or clients, then you would give yourself a paperclip or a poker chip whenever you feel you are assertive. This serves to help increase your self-esteem and make you feel proud that you really are improving your behavior. Giving yourself a token also helps you keep in mind your goal of becoming more assertive. As a result, using tokens can really help increase your self-esteem as you accumulate more and more of them as the day goes by.

You might decide to use tokens as a means to help you get more referrals. At first you could give yourself a token for even thinking about asking a client for a referral. Later on in the week or month, you could give yourself a token only if you actually asked a client for five referrals. And then, later on, you could give yourself a token only if a client actually gave you referrals.

I worked with a securities broker who worked in the California branch of a very prestigious New York-based stock brokerage firm. He had the perpetual problem of being late in the morning.

On the West Coast the stock market opens at 7 in the morning because of the three-hour time difference. My client was not a morning person—he was more of a night owl. He came alive in the late afternoon or evening. But he wanted to get to the office earlier. His tardiness was really an avoidance behavior, a fear symptom.

To combat his fear and change his behavior, every time he got to the office on time, he would give himself a token.

I also had him put one slight modification in his behavioral contract. Every time he got to the office *early*—whether it was only five or ten minutes—he would give himself *two* tokens. Interestingly, he found himself wanting to get to work early not because it was important to his boss but because he wanted to get that token.

A friend of mine is a psychologist who worked with the University of Michigan football team. The University of Michigan Wolverines were in 1986 among the best NCAA college football teams in the country. They're ferocious. Those young men will do anything for their team. They'll practically kill to win a game.

But that Wolverine team was not always as successful. Years ago the Wolverines' psychologist decided that tokens might be an effective tool to help get the players to tackle harder, fumble less, and recover fumbles more frequently.

The coaching staff, on the advice of the psychologist, started putting little stickers on the players' helmets for every big tackle they made or for every fumble they recovered. The ends and the wide receivers received stickers for every catch they made. The coaching staff found that these players would do practically anything to get one of the stickers. They would jump over people, mow people down, practically go through brick walls to get one of those tokens.

When you think about it, if you're on an opposing football team lined up across the scrimmage line from a football player who has a helmet full of stickers, it's a little intimidating. You know that player must have done something right to get all those tokens.

It's a lot like the Army's way of giving stripes to denote rank or valor. For every heroic act, or everything a soldier achieves, he or she gets a little emblem on the uniform. This is an interesting way of receiving tokens. It's basically what our whole reward system in the United States is all about. Recognition through a reward that all can see and admire is often more valued than money, which is itself just another token.

Here's another example of how effective tokens can be. I recently talked to a mother who was having a problem with her son's behavior. Her son would race out of his room in the morning, not picking up any toys, not making his bed, not putting his clothes away.

The mother tried spanking. She tried yelling at the child. But nothing seemed to work for long. Obviously the child would try to avoid punishment by picking up his toys, but that would usually last only about two or three days—certainly not more than a week.

She asked me how to change some of her child's behaviors. I told her very frankly that the child needed a much more physical form of reward than praise and certainly something different from punishment. Since her son liked to play army, I told her to give the child army men as a token reward. She responded, "What if he doesn't do anything that I can reward him for?"

This is a popular misconception. Every child does *something*—however small—that somewhat approximates a behavior you want it to do.

For example, this child *at least* looked at his clothes before he left them and left the room in a shambles. The child *at least* threw all of his toys on top of the bed before he left his room in the morning. I told the mother to reward the child for anything—any behavior—which was even close to what she wanted as a target behavior.

She first started rewarding the child with one army man for just picking up one toy from the floor. Next she rewarded him with a man only for putting the toys away. She then rewarded the child only for throwing clothes into one corner of the room, instead of all over the room. Next she rewarded him with an army man only for putting dirty clothes in the hamper, and then, finally, for hanging up clothes in his closet.

You can see that she was steadily rewarding the child first for things that were close to what she wanted, and ultimately, after two or three weeks, only for exactly what she wanted.

She was surprised not only at how fast this program worked, but also at how long the child continued to pick up his clothes. He didn't go back to his old habits, as he did when she just screamed at him or punished him with a spanking. She randomly rewarded the child with an army man to maintain the habit pattern.

In another case, I had the opportunity to work with someone who was trying to lose weight. One of the toughest things we do as human beings is to decrease our weight once we have set a habit of eating heavily. This individual was around fifty pounds overweight. He told me he exercised, which I doubted. But, more important, he told me he was on a diet that wasn't working.

Well, diets usually do work over a long period of time. But most people will stay on a diet for only about two days and then go back to eating their lemon meringue pie or candy.

The individual I worked with carried poker chips in one of his suit pockets. At first, we had him give himself a token reward of a poker chip every time he *thought* about resisting a high-calorie food. The following week, we *only* rewarded him for eating a salad, or eating food he knew was consistent with his diet. Finally, towards the end of the program, he was *only* rewarded for a whole day of staying on his diet, plus exercising. He gave himself an extra token for exercising.

After the fourth or fifth week, not only would he have a low-calorie drink for breakfast, a salad for lunch, and a low-calorie meal for dinner, he would also have to run one mile during the day. Only if he accomplished those things would he get a token. He did indeed develop a habit of staying on his diet, plus exercising. He lost weight faster using this method than anything else he had tried.

If you are a businessperson, you can use these tokens in your business life. Give yourself a token after every phone call you make or every appointment you book, if that's your target behavior. If you aren't yet at that stage, give yourself a token every time you even *think* about making a phone call or booking an appointment.

With your tailor-made peak performance program you've designed for yourself, you'll be surprised how quickly you can change behaviors so you do exactly what you should do. By sticking to your behavioral contract—giving yourself rewards and tokens when you deserve them and not giving yourself them when you don't deserve them—you'll find that your business will increase dramatically and the target behaviors you want to modify will change faster than you ever thought possible.

Follow your contract as closely as possible. If you have any questions at all, please call me at my office--714-730-3560. Or write me: Dr. Kerry Johnson, P.O. Box 1404, Tustin, California 92681.

Staying on this program for the six- to eight-week period, remembering how you can use conditioning techniques to help you instead of hurt you, and remembering how you can rid yourself of your self-sabotaging fears, will totally and absolutely cause your productivity to skyrocket to heights you never before thought possible.

Use the peak performance selling program. Follow the techniques outlined. You'll be very glad you did.